Ocean, as Much as Rain

Ocean, as Much as Rain

STORIES, LYRICAL PROSE, AND POEMS FROM TIBET

Tsering Woeser

EDITED AND TRANSLATED FROM THE CHINESE BY
Fiona Sze-Lorrain with Dechen Pemba

FOREWORD BY
Pankaj Mishra

Duke University Press   *Durham and London*   2026

Project Editor: Bird Williams
Designed by Dave Rainey
Typeset in Warnock Pro and Matrix II by Copperline
Book Services

Library of Congress Cataloging-in-Publication Data
Names: Weise, [date] author | Sze-Lorrain, Fiona editor
translator | Pemba, Dechen editor translator | Mishra, Pankaj
writer of foreword
Title: Ocean, as much as rain : stories, lyrical prose, and
poems from Tibet / by Tsering Woeser ; edited and translated
from the Chinese by Fiona Sze-Lorrain and Dechen Pemba ;
foreword by Pankaj Mishra.
Description: Durham : Duke University Press, 2026. |
Includes bibliographical references and index.
Identifiers: LCCN 2025021833 (print)
LCCN 2025021834 (ebook)
ISBN 9781478033110 paperback
ISBN 9781478029687 hardcover
ISBN 9781478061861 ebook
Subjects: LCSH: Tibet Autonomous Region (China)—Fiction |
Tibet Autonomous Region (China)—Poetry | Tibet Autonomous
Region (China)—Foreign relations—China | LCGFT: Short
stories | Poetry | Essays | Fiction.
Classification: LCC PL2966.O47 A2 2026 (print)
LCC PL2966. O47 (ebook)
LC record available at https://lccn.loc.gov/2025021833
LC ebook record available at https://lccn.loc.gov/2025021834

Cover art: Tenzing Rigdol, *Biography of a Thought* (detail),
2022–24, acrylic on stretched canvas and woven carpet
© Tenzing Rigdol

All photos, except those on pages 77, 79, 113 (fair use) or unless
otherwise indicated, are courtesy of Tsering Woeser

CONTENTS

FOREWORD

Pankaj Mishra

One late December evening in 2007, a few hours before boarding the new Chinese train to Lhasa, I met Woeser at a hotel in Beijing. I remember she spoke with passion about what she saw as a colonial imposition, which spelled the end of Tibetan culture. And the more I learned of her background, the more impressed and moved I was.

Very little in her life had predisposed her to the role of the "dissident," or the prominent critic of the Chinese presence in Tibet. Her half-Tibetan father had been a teenage soldier in China's People's Liberation Army (PLA) that "peacefully liberated" Tibet in 1951, establishing Communist rule over the country's largely Buddhist population. Born in 1966, Woeser herself, as she writes in one of her poems, was "raised under the bugle of the PLA" in Tibet, and indoctrinated deeply enough as a child to burst into tears on hearing of Mao's death in 1976.

As a young poet, she had, she told me, no interest in politics until she read, in the late 1980s, a Chinese translation of a book on Tibetan exiles by John Avedon, son of the famous photographer Richard Avedon. She had been shocked when her father and uncle, also a dedicated Tibetan Communist, confirmed that at least 60 to 70 percent of the book's account of Chinese atrocities against Tibetans was true. But it was not until 2000, when she met her husband Wang Lixiong, the leading Han Chinese writer on Tibet, that she began to write about Tibetan politics.

In 2003, Chinese authorities banned her most popular book, *Notes on Tibet*, ostensibly for praising the Dalai Lama; they also fired her from her job as editor of *Tibetan Literature* and forbade her from leaving the country. Ordered to receive "reeducation" at one of the railway's construction sites, Woeser left Tibet and now lives with Wang Lixiong in Beijing. Her life as a freelance writer remains precarious: Chinese internet police frequently shut down her blogs.

Translated by Fiona Sze-Lorrain with Dechen Pemba, *Ocean, as Much as Rain* introduces us to a writer who in isolation has developed a startling range of skills. Memoirist, poet, fictionist, historian, critic, and polemicist: She assumes these different roles with serene confidence, style, and wit. Flourishing in profoundly unpromising circumstances, Woeser ennobles the free life of the mind like few writers today.

OCEAN CAN BE RAIN

Woeser's Poetry, Fiction, and Lyrical Prose

Fiona Sze-Lorrain

As an artist and a bilingual, educated, courageous Tibetan woman, Tsering Woeser (ཚེ་རིང་འོད་ཟེར།) is uniquely positioned to observe and comment on her society and world. Popularly known by the single name "Woeser," she has authored more than twenty collections of poetry, fiction, and nonfiction, including two of the most significant Chinese-language books on Tibet: *Notes on Tibet* (2003) and *Forbidden Memory: Tibet During the Cultural Revolution* (2006). Woeser has earned worldwide respect as much for her prolific literary work as for her sociopolitical engagement as a dissident within the borders of the current People's Republic of China. As a poet, essayist, fiction writer, and journalist, she is one of the few Tibetans who works across various literary genres. As a human rights activist, she crosses firewalls, speaking out while being physically contained inside mainland China.

Born on July 21, 1966, in Lhasa, Woeser grew up mostly in the Kham region of Tibet (in today's Sichuan province). Her father, Tsering Dorje, had been recruited into the People's Liberation Army (PLA) in 1950 at age thirteen as Mao Zedong marched his army toward Lhasa. His position as a PLA officer and senior commander afforded Woeser an elite Chinese upbringing and education unavailable to most Tibetans. Her upbringing was stable, her family environment comfortable, with the period of China's opening up in the 1980s as a backdrop in which there were few political tensions or divisions.

Woeser graduated in 1988 with a degree in Chinese from Southwest University for Nationalities in Chengdu, Sichuan. She quickly found work as a journalist and an editor at *Kardze Daily*, the local newspaper in Dartsedo,[1] the capital of Tibetan Autonomous Prefecture, Kardze.[2] In 1990, she returned to Lhasa, where she served as an editor for the government-run journal *Tibetan Literature*. It was then that she experienced an existential awakening. This, in addition to her father's death a year later, made her feel for the first time "sinicized," she later recalled. The anguish of becoming an alien in her own hometown left her with an acute feeling of emptiness along with her grief.

Educated solely in Chinese, Woeser began to grow fully conscious of her Tibetan identity. Her sociocultural coming-of-age in the early 1990s led to a heightened political awareness that was later found in her cross-genre writing. Woeser therefore writes as both an outsider and insider in all senses. On top of being discriminated against by her Chinese peers as an "ethnic minority writer," she felt alienated from her own Tibetan selfhood through her marriage to a Han Chinese man in 2004, to say nothing of the guilt of not knowing the Tibetan language well enough to express herself in writing. Tibetan-language education was not an option for anyone of her generation.

It took her years to break free from the confines of writing only in Chinese. Doing so enabled her to leverage her native language to reaffirm her Tibetan identity and speak out against physical repression. She calls her residence in Beijing a kind of "exile" away from Lhasa, which she had felt compelled to leave. Still, it is with this conflicting sense of cultural liminality that Woeser has written so movingly about the dilemmas often experienced by Tibetans, who must negotiate and cohabitate with their Chinese "friends," as well as their "savage" religious rites, "primitive" customs, and long-standing taboos and superstitions, all of which remain much misunderstood not only by the foreigners and the Chinese but also by the younger and sinicized generation of Tibetans.

Apart from her journalism and editorial work, Woeser began publishing poems in the late 1980s as a bridge to other genres. Poetry was her first passport to a literary life. The subject matter of her work became increasingly political, addressing controversial topics such as the status of Tibet, its Buddhist culture and contemporary past. As one of the few Tibetan writers who have no choice but to use Chinese as their language of expression, Woeser routinely refers to this linguistic anomaly as her lifelong "tongue surgery" or "linguistic mutation." Such phrases are rarely voiced by "minority" writers in China, because they are viewed as subversive in a despotic one-party regime that cracks down on any sign of civil dissent.

After her college years, Woeser found peers from the regional writing circle to share her artistic tastes and inspirations. She has named Russian poets Anna Akhmatova and Marina Tsvetaeva as her poetic heroines throughout her writing life. In her younger days, she read the modernist British and American canon and was attracted to countercultural figures such as Allen

Ginsberg, even though state-endorsed establishments would consider these foreign cultural influences elitist if not radical.

Woeser reads very little Chinese contemporary writing nowadays. This is both her personal and political choice, a continuation of her own decolonization process. She explains, "The reason I don't read contemporary Chinese writing is precisely because there are very few Chinese writers, poets, and scholars who dare to criticize totalitarianism in China today; almost all of them pander to the authorities. There are very few intellectuals in the true sense of the word in this country, plus the vast majority of Chinese writers, poets, scholars are cultural hegemonists. This is what my life experience as a Tibetan surviving in China has taught me." Instead, she often immerses herself in translations of poets and writers from the former Soviet Union or countries that have also suffered a history of totalitarianism. Woeser cites philosopher Hannah Arendt's *The Origins of Totalitarianism* (1951) and Russian American cultural theorist Svetlana Boym's *The Future of Nostalgia* (2002) as two of the most influential books in her reading life. An aficionado of Franz Kafka and Jorge Luis Borges, she continues to revisit Marguerite Duras's books and films for her appealing style of narration and considers Jean-Paul Sartre a spiritual guide. Woeser's Buddhist practice is an unassailable impetus in her writing. "Whenever I can, I read and recite prayers: *The Heart Sutra, Ksitigarbha Sutra, Tara Sutra . . .*" she shared in a personal email. "I meditate and commit myself to two hundred and sixteen full-body prostrations every night. Like osmosis, such discipline must have impacted my writing."

As Woeser gained more recognition in China in the mid-1990s, her poems rejected a romanticized self and became more narrative. She branched out into more hybrid prose, specifically investigative writing. During an interview with the online international journal *Cerise Press* in 2012, the poet described in retrospect those changes as part of a process that had allowed her to "slowly actualize the self-expression of a 'Tibetan identity.'" Moving back to Lhasa at age twenty-four—and getting to see and know Tibet with her own eyes—led the much-sinicized Woeser to both a spiritual and personal identity crisis, which she reconfirmed as the overarching conduit for her political fiction and journalism in subsequent years. When her best-selling book of lyrical prose *Notes on Tibet* was released in early 2003, it was banned and condemned by the Chinese government due to its "forbidden subject matter." Her publisher in Guangzhou claimed to have selected her manuscript for publication because of its beautiful language and artistic merits.

But the editor did not even know who and what the Dalai Lama was. This is a glimpse into the sociopolitical climate of the post-Tiananmen China, whose suppression of politically "problematic" periods, incidents, and individuals had removed them all from the collective memory and replaced them with a focus on economic prosperity and development.

Following the book ban, Woeser faced aggressive persecution and immediate censorship. She was ordered to self-criticize and confess. But she put an end to the situation in a letter dated September 14, 2003, to the highest authorities at *Tibetan Literature*, in which she refused to confess, refused the reeducation, and moved into exile in Beijing. As a result, she was summarily fired from her job, was cut off from access to social welfare, and had her passport denied. Short of being thrown into prison, she was deprived of everything that could be taken away. To this day, Woeser has had every application for a passport turned down; she even resorted in 2008 to suing the Chinese government—unsuccessfully—for denying her her basic rights as a citizen. Since then, she has declared herself an independent writer and blogger, and continues to be one of the most eloquent critics of the Chinese violence, political oppression, and cultural suppression in Tibet.

Woeser was an early internet user among Tibetans. She kept two blogs in Chinese that were widely read by Tibetan and Chinese netizens. When the Chinese government shut both blogs down in 2006, she launched blogs hosted on overseas servers to evade censorship and control. One of them, *Map of Maroon Red*, came of age during the months of Tibetan uprising in 2008 and was a leading source of information for primary news about Tibet. In a time before social media and mobile phone apps became common, the blog featured Woeser's daily updates, an invaluable resource for firsthand news when the whole of Tibet was under an information blackout.

The *Map of Maroon Red* blog was receiving 3 million hits while being translated into English by *China Digital Times*. Woeser soon became the target of Chinese nationalist hackers. A group known as Red Hackers destroyed the blog in May 2008, and all its original posts were lost. Around this time, her Skype account was also hacked and her phones tapped. The next incarnation of her blog was *Invisible Tibet* (http://woeser.middle-way.net/), which remains active. Woeser uses it to religiously document the next wave of protests that spread across Tibet: the self-immolation protests that began in 2009, peaked in 2012, and sporadically continue. Images and short videos she frequently posts are a mosaic of personal activities, funny everyday observations, reflections on world news such as the war in Ukraine, and reposts from Tibetan exile activities and beautiful landscapes, accompanied by short captions. Other than maintaining her blogs and social media accounts, Woeser is a regular opinion contributor to Radio Free Asia, with her commentary pieces published and broadcast in both Tibetan and Chinese. Not even the pandemic could stop her from blogging and posting on Instagram.

The most active Tibetan blogger of our time, Woeser furnishes uncensored resources about the contemporary situation in Tibet. But she does not report from an insular, time-bound perspective. She does so with an eye on history and current international affairs. To some extent, she is idealistic about her mission as writer. In her book *Voices from Tibet* (2014), she describes the experience of giving "voice through as many channels as possible—books, blogs, radio programs, Twitter [now X], Facebook and press interviews" as tantamount to a "one-woman media" outlet and a testament to the fact that "for the powerless, the pen can be wielded as a weapon, a weapon honed by the Tibetan faith, tradition and culture." Her social media presence now cannot be undermined socially and politically: In spite of heavy censorship and disinformation, she has almost 150,000 followers on X and a solid presence on Facebook and Instagram, all handled by herself with no marketing, publicity, or outreach management, no digital strategy or outside funding. She is also the most translated and read author on the highly profiled *High Peaks Pure Earth*, a website that offers translations, news, and commentary from Tibetan cyberspace. In 2022, *High Peaks Pure Earth* translated and published all of Woeser's Instagram posts, depicting almost on a daily basis Lhasa's eerie descent into a draconian COVID lockdown.

Woeser's sustained, sometimes even round-the-clock online presence demonstrates the considerable influence she wields in shaping international opinions of Tibetan identity and broadcasting the realities of life in present-day Tibet. Yet her work is more subtle and subversive than straightforward noncompliance or opposition: It is the voice of an educated witness who has been silenced as a "Chinese subject of Tibetan ethnicity," only to be made louder as a Tibetan locked within China proper. Her insistence on freely leaving her home in hard-line Beijing to visit Chinese-ruled Lhasa as an unauthorized journalist is a creative response that mobilizes her dissent as well as her relationship to geography and centralized state-led apparatus. As conveyed in her travel accounts and *Dossier* (2014), Chinese filmmaker Zhu Rikun's documentary about Woeser's closely policed life in Beijing and Tibet, it is logistically and emotionally onerous for Woeser—or any unpoliced Tibetan—to enter Tibet. Yet instead of being estranged from Tibet or the Tibetans, Woeser is drawn closer to them from Beijing. Despite being a "person of interest" ordered to "disappear" or stay out of Beijing "from time to time," she has found ways to stay visible, continuing to own her facts, timeline, and the events she documents.

Woeser is married to Wang Lixiong (b. 1953), an influential Chinese writer and intellectual whose arguments unusually steer clear of ideology and whose sympathy for the Tibetan cause is not without criticism of Tibetans themselves. Thirteen years Woeser's senior, Wang appears in his wife's writing either anonymously or specifically identified. His own work includes science fiction, along with essays and scholarship on ecological or environmental concerns and cultural and racial subjugation in China. Both Woeser and Wang have been friends with leading activist-artists and intellectuals, including Ai Weiwei (b. 1957; now in exile), Hu Jia (b. 1973; frequently placed under house arrest), and Ilham Tohti (b. 1969; now serving life imprisonment). In the *New York Review of Books*, the Pulitzer Prize–winning journalist Ian Johnson describes the couple as "two of China's best-known thinkers on the government's policy toward ethnic minorities." Woeser is among the first signatories, with the late Liu Xiaobo, of "Charter 08." Often placed under house arrest during "sensitive public occasions," she is still living under close police surveillance in Beijing, Lhasa, and whenever she travels. Just after the pandemic outbreak in 2020, she was staying in Beijing. Later, though, she was able to return to Lhasa, where, just as the city was going into a harsh lockdown in August 2022, her mother, Tsering Youdon, passed away after an illness. When we reworked parts of this introduction in December 2022, China was lifting its zero-COVID policy, and Woeser was still in Lhasa for the foreseeable future.

Woeser's work has received several international recognitions, including a nomination for the 2007 Neustadt International Prize for Literature, and been published into many languages. One of her nonfiction titles, *Forbidden Memory: Tibet During the Cultural Revolution*, was awarded the 2006 *China Times* Top Ten Best Chinese Books Award in Taiwan. She has received two Hellman/Hammett International Grants, the 2007 Freedom of Expression Prize from the Norwegian Authors' Union, and the "Fearless Speaker" Medal from the Association of Tibetan Journalists in India. Other honors include the 2009 Lin Zhao Memorial Prize from the Independent Chinese PEN Center, the 2010 Courage in Journalism Prize from the International Women's Media Foundation, and the Prince Claus Award in 2011. In 2013, the US State Department conferred on Woeser an International Women of Courage Award, which was presented by then–First Lady Michelle Obama and then–Secretary of State John Kerry in the writer's absence.

Despite Woeser's recognition as a representative literary figure and moral voice of the Tibetans in mainland China, very little if any of her fiction, auto-fiction, and lyrical prose has been translated into English. Little is known about her humor and mischief as a storyteller. Even less is known about her cinematic descriptions of ancient townships and landscapes in Kham or the dramatic and gossipy Tibetan wives from those bittersweet love stories she wrote during her years as a journalist. For the past three decades, particularly since her persecution and house arrests, as well as the 2008 Tibetan uprisings, Woeser's eloquent literary voice has been sidelined by her more political writings and online journalism. Among the latter, 2020 saw the English translation of the book she wrote in 2006, titled *Forbidden Memory: Tibet During the Cultural Revolution*. The book contains eleven galleries of monochrome photographs taken by her father between approximately 1964 and 1976, as well as color photos taken by Woeser herself from 2001 to 2004.

Two earlier books translated into English, *Tibet on Fire: Self-Immolation Against Chinese Rule* (2016) and *Voices from Tibet* (2014), center on the more recent political struggles and resistance of Tibetans living in China. Since 2003, all of Woeser's fiction and poetry have been banned by the Chinese authorities. Even though she is able to find mainstream publication in Taiwan, it has become increasingly difficult for her to reach readers in other Sinophone areas, including the heavily oppressed "post–Umbrella Revolution" Hong Kong. Yet the honesty, acuity, and urgency of her activism implies that her literary aesthetics commands attention in its own right, even more so when Woeser regards herself as a poet and writer first and foremost.

Between memoir, fiction, and travelogue, *Ocean, as Much as Rain* is the first translated volume of Woeser's lyrical prose, stories, reportage, and poems in English. Woeser wrote the earliest piece in 2001 and has revised the latest addition in 2015 and 2016. This new collection consists of a short autobiographical piece and eight long narratives that oscillate between absurdity and realism, autobiography and testament, anecdotal reminiscence and historical sketch, meditation and cynical confession. I first began working with Woeser in 2011, and Dechen Pemba joined me on this project in 2016. Since then, both of us have worked in close collaboration and consultation with the author on multiple fronts. The choice of *Ocean, as Much as Rain* as the title of our book came to me because of its all-encompassing lyricism and implications. I have selected and curated the work presented here as well as translated them, four of which (prose pieces) are cotranslations. For the purpose of clarity, the translation credits are indicated separately before the opening poem. I edited the prose work with my colleague Dechen Pemba, who responded to my queries and provided at least two paragraphs and important input for this introductory essay in addition to its shared editing. We also provided endnotes where necessary, in addition to translating and revising the author's notes.

Interspersed with these translated prose writings are selected poems by Tsering Woeser in my translation, of which two new pieces were originally completed in 2022. In her narratives, Woeser the narrator and protagonist recounts the fabulous lives and stories of lamas; a sky-burial master; a veteran Gar musician; an antiques dealer and businessman who promotes environmentalism, sets up a private Tibetan heritage museum, and runs, all by himself, a grassroots ecological campaign . . . These are just some of the ordinary yet otherworldly Tibetans whom Woeser has encountered during her various travels in Chinese-ruled Tibet. Through them, more crucially, she reveals an imperiled people, culture, thought, and way of life. Although Woeser seems to present herself as a character like others, she comes across as a spontaneous Brechtian raconteur who knows how to convey her skepticism and criticism of the Chinese state ideologies in an oblique but artful manner. What is therefore atypical of Woeser's narrative style is how each piece shifts whimsically in a borderland of objective and subjective realities, within their larger allegories and backstories, as well as a broader relevance. These heartbreaking chronicles also present strange and peculiar situations that challenge each personage to react humanely, sometimes against their spiritual truth.

À la W. G. Sebald and Svetlana Alexievich, Woeser's prose interweaves photographs, reportage, drama, and documentary details in an autofiction. Her voice is elegiac, provocative, polyphonic, and beautifully digressive. Earlier, in her epilogue for *Voices from Tibet*, she states, "As a writer, I have found my conviction to write coming into focus gradually: To write is to experience; to write is to pray; to write is to bear witness. Experience, prayer and bearing witness all intertwine. And to bear witness is to give voice." Bearing witness is a timeless writerly ambition and vision, once pursued by literary giants like Aleksandr Solzhenitsyn, who finds in literature his responsibility for history. In this respect, Woeser is no less sincere about her role as storyteller. Charged with pathos and emotion, her language embraces anxiety and the untranslatables by using humor to talk seriously. In each of these stories, she uses her personal archive of photographs, brings alive characters who would otherwise be unknown or forgotten, revives places from the long-lost childhoods of her parents, and confronts wild nature as well as cultural sites defeated by money, tourism, and pollution. She questions the ruins, monasteries, and unvisited quarters in Tibet about their present and future. What better response to ruins and transcendence in the context of a long history of political erasure than in words and pictures from a specific time?

Few contemporary writers in Chinese language approach Tibet without self-censorship or orientalism. Does this have anything to do with Chinese as the medium of expression, its inherent linguistic and cultural colonization engineering the "irony"? Tsering Woeser is possibly the only woman as well as Tibetan to do so in the current political climate. But as a raconteur she is less interested in being prescient than in being relevant. Above all, she is realistic about her vulnerability as a political artist, which is why in her fiction we can catch a glimpse of her frustrations, grievances, and unanswerable prayers. For her, to write is to "experience," to "pray," and to "bear witness," and all three intertwine in her work as quest for higher truths. Ultimately these manifest in an attempt to survive and think and act, but not retaliate.

An example can be seen in her postscript to "Let Me Write, the Fear of Lhasa Breaks My Heart," a poem she wrote after being forced to leave Lhasa in the wake of the 2008 Beijing Summer Olympic Games, after her traumatizing ordeal of being detained, interrogated, and humiliated for eight hours. In it Woeser simply and powerfully writes, "You have guns, I have a pen." Even in such moments when she has nothing else on her, she thinks of the pen as a weapon for peace, a tool of resistance, a shield. During those seven days of physical and emotional anguish, Woeser kept a secret diary. An excerpt—the first entry—is translated and published here for the first time in English. Today this diary stands as a personal and eloquent "document" of "missing history," to borrow the words from Alexievich: It is an extraordinary testimony of a lucid Tibetan writer who brings to light the dark, unuttered events, the uprising in Lhasa before and during the "glorious" Beijing Olympics that historic year.

Yet never once in *Ocean, as Much as Rain* has the author sought to deliberately aestheticize violence or monumentalize what's lost for art's sake, even if doing so might help her engage a larger and consensual mainstream audience who wants to embrace a Shangri-la fantasy. With an imaginative use of satire, parody, and self-deprecation, Woeser does not give up hope of transcending the censorship levied against her writing and citizenship. Through her stories, poems, texts, images, she strives to renew her own sense of artistic freedom by writing, both poetically and politically, from the complex workings of oral history, collective memory, myths, and personal secrets. Ever mindful but unafraid of her—and our—contesting stream of consciousness, she redefines freedom in more ways than one, undaunted by the unknown that her writing and life may reveal.

Paris, February 2017
Revised—February 2023, September/December 2024, January 2025

NOTES

1. Kangding in Chinese.
2. Ganzi in Chinese.

TRANSLATION CREDITS

"My Tongue Surgery," "Celebrity Street Toilets in Lhasa," "The Ruins of Lhasa: Yabzhi Taktser," "Back to Lhasa, Day One, *from* Seven Days in Lhasa," and "The Killing Trip" are translated by Fiona Sze-Lorrain.

"Rinchen the Sky-Burial Master," "Garpon La's Offerings," and the author interview "An Eye from History and Reality: Woeser and Her Story of Tibet" are translated by Dechen Pemba and Fiona Sze-Lorrain.

"The King of *Dzi*" and "Ocean, as Much as Rain" are translated by Fiona Sze-Lorrain and Dechen Pemba.

The poems are translated by Fiona Sze-Lorrain.

1

A Sheet of Paper Can Also Become a Knife

A sheet of paper can also become a knife
even sharper
I only wanted to turn the page over
but my right ring finger—cut
Although the wound was small
blood oozed thinly
Pain was slight
This metamorphosis startled me
Even paper can suddenly become a knife
What error
or turning point makes it possible?
I'm in awe of this plain paper

October 16, 2007—Beijing

2

My Tongue Surgery

In the early spring of 1981, I graduated from junior high school in an increasingly sinicized town called Kangding in eastern Tibet.[1] As it happened, the Southwest University for Nationalities in Sichuan was recruiting Tibetan students for its foundational preparatory program. An equivalent to the Chinese high school program, this course of study was launched in 1985 and aimed to accelerate cultural assimilation. It proved to be a successful experiment in Tibetan classes and former secondary schools in numerous cities including Beijing and Shanghai. Of course, the unanimous official justification for such program was "to help Tibet groom talent."

I enrolled in the program out of my own will, and certainly without coaxing from my parents. In the heat of my rebellion, I had no desire to let them restrain or control my life. Hardly aware of any difference between a Han Chinese place and a Tibetan district, I thought of Chengdu as a huge city full of thrilling novelties. Neither did I anticipate myself becoming gradually alienated from my own homeland and its culture.

Clad in his military uniform, Father sent me off to Chengdu. We took a long-distance bus ride, and on stiff seats rode over the towering Mount Erlang. (What is it called in Tibetan?) Past the mountain, the scenery outside was rich with greenery: crisp bamboos, large patches of vegetable lands, and branches lavished with fruits. Once we alighted, I was greeted with a pot before a street eatery, stuffed with lonely cooked rabbit heads that exuded an alluring smell. I was stunned and immediately thought of a Tibetan folk legend, how one turned harelipped when one consumed rabbit meat. Right before my eyes, a path meandering through mountains and valleys emerged, and a rabbit we call *ribong* in Tibetan suddenly vanished along the way.

Much of what awaited me was an exotic contrast to my old life in Kangding. Cuisine, clothes, accents . . . I started to indulge in braised eel in soy sauce, spicy rabbit heads, and frog legs. Aware of having violated taboos, I was made more aware of coming across as a superstitious "barbarian" had I not tried these dishes. Locals in Chengdu seemed to enjoy calling others "barbarians": If you chickened out of eating rabbit heads, you were bound to be an idiotic barbarian. Chengdu is a humid basin. My Tibetan classmates and I were surprised when we woke up with our hair heavily curled. Most of the locals tended to stereotype such curls as a unique trait of ethnic minorities. So every morning we would violently comb our long, curly hair until it turned straight, and eventually trimmed it to ear length. Although our hair remained curly, it looked permed: We now each resembled a middle-aged woman in the streets of Chengdu.

Our foundational program was no more than a "tiny department" sealed off from the rest of the university. We took our lessons in two spacious classrooms in a corner of the campus and did not get to interact with the local students. In fact, we had no idea what they were learning, even though they shared our age. I imagined they must be following the same curriculum: After all, our textbooks were identical to theirs, nor did we have the chance to own a textbook in the Tibetan or Yi script. There were about seventy of us in all, with ages ranging from fourteen to sixteen. Most of us were Tibetan, some ethnic Yi. Only a smattering few spoke Tibetan or the Yi language. With time, all of us became fluent in the Chengdu dialect.

Nine years later, upon my return to Lhasa from Kangding, I realized the extent of changes that had occurred in me and how they took on a certain profound significance. Relatives in Lhasa described my tongue as one "after surgery," because when it came to traditional phonetics in Tibetan—trills, retroflex consonants, or alveolar consonants—I was as ignorant as any foreigner. I could do no more than produce odd sounds, let alone say words aloud. I couldn't even pronounce "Lhasa" properly in Tibetan.

My university experience was no less than an existential displacement. Over thirty minority nationalities, each with a distinct name, had enrolled in the entire Southwest University for Nationalities. While we seemed to live in harmony in a multiethnic setting, we failed to understand the history and culture of our various ethnic nationalities. We were taught the diverse ethnic festive meals, the songs and dances that tribes savored when drinking around the bonfire, and that was it. Once in a while, we would splash water over one another as a way of celebrating the Dai people's Songkran festival. Although the "highlights" of a multicultural milieu instilled in me an acute awareness of my "Tibetan" plight at all times, none of us had ever received an authentic ethnic education.

I was capable of writing long eloquent speeches about Emperor Qin, who built the Great Wall of China, yet I knew nothing of the Potala Palace and its construction. I could memorize Tang poems and Song verses from back to front, but understood none of the poetry by the Sixth Dalai Lama Tsangyang Gyatso. I knew the stories of revolutionary martyrs in Red China inside out, yet had no inkling of our own heroes from the 1959 Lhasa uprising . . . Fortunately, I did not forget Lhasa, my birthplace. Since moving with my parents to eastern Tibet at the age of four, I carried with me a profound nostalgia and homesickness. It was only in the spring of 1990, a year after my college graduation, that I finally found the chance to return to Lhasa, serving as an editor for the state-run literary journal *Tibetan Literature*.

What I saw and experienced upon arriving in Lhasa astonished me. Childhood memories now a blur, I could only grapple with vague impressions of

Lhasa from my father's vintage photographs: How marvelous and timeless the capital city was. But the reality was nothing close to its history: Armed soldiers flooded the city, and military armored cars rumbled on while they ran over boulevards. In March 1989, many Tibetans including monks, nuns, and civilians took to the streets to protest against the Chinese government's oppression of Tibetans in 1959. In retaliation, Beijing declared martial law in Lhasa for a year and seven months.

As I stood on the soil of Lhasa, a deep solitude swelled within me. No doubt this had something to do with my tongue surgery. I could hardly speak a complete sentence in Tibetan. Whatever I blurted out was none other than the standardized Mandarin with a Sichuan accent. My mother tongue is not Chinese: It had been displaced during my adolescence. I even wondered if my appearance had also changed drastically, since I had greedily eaten spicy rabbit heads and violated various taboos.

Another twenty years passed before I returned to Lhasa as someone who had lost herself. My self-pursuit, resistance, and the ensuing acceptance ... ultimately to narrate stories of Tibet from my perspective today, took too long. In the end, no one can deny that these words I write are also written in the Chinese language. This is a fact that will forever sadden me. But all things in the universe exist for a reason: There must be a reason why I was and have been a displaced self. As the Tibetan saying goes, *It is but predestiny when a bird falls on a rock.* Thank goodness my heart wasn't replaced.

I will never forget my first visit to Jokhang Temple. It signifies a vital turning point in my life, and like a powerful electric current, it steadily impacted my "dissimilated" self. It was dusk. My relatives, still preserving their Tibetan customs, brought me to the temple. For no reason, tears streamed from my eyes once I entered the sacred site. When I set eyes on the statue of the smiling Buddha, I couldn't help but wail with grief. An inner voice spoke out to me, *You're home at last,* before it was overwhelmed by a pang of pain: A monk nearby was sighing in Tibetan, *How pitiful this gyamo is.*[2]

2007, Lhasa
Revised—March 2014, Beijing

NOTES

1. In Tibetan, Kangding is called Dartsedo.
2. In Tibetan, a *gyamo* refers to a Han Chinese girl. [author's note]

3

Spring

Spring is here
spring in Lhasa
Every afternoon, ruined valleys
will stir sandstorms
Butter lamps from the Johkang
blaze in our hands every day

Spring is here
spring in Lhasa
Every day, the surrounding barracks
will sound the bugle a few times
My old mother
circumambulates every day around the Potala

O, spring in Lhasa
spring in Lhasa . . .
Just like this, spring is over one by one

Losar (Tibetan New Year) 2004, Lhasa

4

Rinchen the Sky-Burial Master

Anyone writing about a sky-burial master is sure to be suspected of having chosen a sensational subject just to gain attention. When one brings up sky burials, all kinds of exotic stereotypes about Tibet leap to mind. Then, if one mentions a sky-burial master, one imagines a uniquely Tibetan practitioner, whose profession involves something between a weird science of dissection and witchcraft. Even the photographs of sky-burial masters that can be found easily on the internet do not reveal much information. For example, there are well-known images from the 1980s taken at the sky-burial site near Lhasa's Sera Monastery. In one of the photographs, a solemn-looking Tibetan man is holding a broad-bladed knife and standing over a tangle of body parts; the bloody flesh only vaguely resembles a human corpse. The scene looks like a bizarre, open-air surgery. Anyone with a sensitive nature would be thoroughly shocked by the images.

The friend who sent me the links to those photographs is a poet who has traveled to Tibet many times, even though he is from south of the Yangtze River. He asked me a little nervously, "Is it possible that all you Tibetans want burials like that when you die?"

Frankly, I had to think hard about how to answer him, because it's not something that can be explained in just a few sentences. It's fairly simple, of course, to describe in a literal way what happens at a traditional sky burial, and many of those kinds of descriptions have been written. There is even a well-known poem that praises the vultures that eat the corpses . . . You can imagine the thrill that people with romanticized ideas about Tibetans get when they read such things. For them, the knife-wielding sky-burial master has the aura of a mystical person with the power to unite the opposing cosmic principles of yin and yang. In reality, though, being a sky-burial master is not something that just anyone would want to do or could do. To be a sky-burial master, you need the courage to bloody your hands with the harsh evidence of life's impermanence, without ever losing your sense of deep compassion.

In Tibet or, more accurately, in all Tibetan areas—it is necessary to make this distinction so readers will not think I mean only the official Tibet Autonomous Region—a sky-burial master is simply a layperson in one's hometown who helps people on their way to reincarnation. His skills and tools are the same as a butcher's, so he has a low social status despite being someone whom everyone needs and comes into contact with eventually. When we die, we need lamas, but we also need a *tokden*.[1]

I remember the time I was staying in Palyul, in Baiyu County. Every morning I would get up early and go to the beautiful Palyul Monastery, built against the base of the mountain, and stay there until dusk. In fact, I was there so often that I almost became the full-time cook for Karma Kuchen Rinpoche, the current Throne Holder of the Palyul Lineage. My culinary skills aren't that great, but I can cook up a pretty good dish of potatoes and beef. You just need to have the courage to throw in lots of chili, Sichuan peppers, and other spices, then heat them all together in a big pot. After a while, you have a really spicy and fragrant dish. I like to tell myself that even now the *draba*—the ordinary monks—and Karma Kuchen Rinpoche cherish the memory of me as the one who always made their mouths burn.

When I was at Dabpa County's Pangpu Monastery, instead of being the cook, I took cooking lessons from Drongkar. You would never imagine that a monk could make such amazing steamed buns: very big and white, and delicious with butter tea. The tsampa that Drongkar kneaded was even better than his steamed buns. In Lhasa, the barley flour for tsampa is ground very fine, using water-powered millstones or machines. But in Kham, the barley flour is ground by hand, so it is coarser. As a result, Kham's tsampa has a stronger barley taste.

The day I departed from Pangpu Monastery, with the intention of going to Dartsedo, Drongkar saw me waiting for the bus on the main road near the monastery. As he was helping me load my backpack, he stuffed some things into my pocket. I tried to see what they were, but he insisted that I not look until I had left. After a while, when the bus was some distance down the road, I reached in my pocket and saw that he had given me *chinden*, Tibetan Buddhist medicine. I tried to look back at the maroon walls of the monastery, but they had disappeared from view. I felt around in my pocket again and discovered that Drongkar had also given me a fifty-yuan note.[2] I almost cried. I knew that he was poor, and his gift showed how wholeheartedly he wanted me to become a true pilgrim.

The bus took me to Nyakchuka. My reason for traveling there was related to a letter from Chodrak, a man from Nyakchuka who had written to me about meeting an authentic sky-burial master. Those few sentences had piqued my curiosity. (You should notice that my stopover in Nyakchuka, en route to Dartsedo, shows how frugal and practical I am when I travel, stopping wherever I please—in the true spirit of "on the road.") I discovered that Chodrak was tall, handsome, and youthful, with curly hair and black eyes.

"Do you want to get to know Tokden Rinchen?" he asked me shortly after we met. "I can take you to see him."

"A *tokden*? What's so special about that?" I replied. "I didn't travel all the way from Lhasa to Kham to see a *tokden*. Lhasa has plenty of *tokdens*. What do you take me for," I added somewhat brusquely, "one of those inland-China types who come to Tibet to see exotic, occult things?"

Chodrak simply smiled. "This *tokden* is unlike any you've ever met; he's a civil servant, head of the livestock protection department."

Eventually, Chodrak and I traveled to the Horra grasslands, and to the livestock disease prevention office—actually just a small lodge—where Tokden Rinchen worked. I have a keen sense of smell, and when Rinchen came in, cordially bringing me a nice hot cup of butter tea, I noticed his peculiar odor. I can't say for sure that all sky-burial masters carry this scent. In any case, I had no choice but to accept the tea and make small talk. I had noticed a portrait of Chairman Mao hanging on the wall. It was the familiar portrait that we had all grown up with. Next to Rinchen's bed was a small wooden box covered by a thin felt cloth and draped with a *khata*, a traditional ceremonial scarf. On the box was a figure of Shakyamuni [the historical Buddha]. Next to the figure was an offering of two freshly plucked wildflowers.

"Rinchen," I asked, "what exactly do you believe in?" I knew the question was complicated, and his answer surprised me.

"During the day," he said, "I believe in Chairman Mao; once the sun goes down, I believe in our Bodhisattvas."

I gave him a perplexed look, then he burst out laughing, proud of himself for having teased me. His joke made me forget about the cup of butter tea I had cautiously put on the table without tasting. I was still wrestling with the fact that the tea had been made by a sky-burial master. (But wait, I'm getting way ahead of myself in telling the story of how I met Rinchen.)

In Nyakchuka, Chodrak had been the head of the county religious affairs bureau, and I never imagined that one day he would become the head of the

county tourism bureau. Indeed, the tourism industry suited him. I should mention that it was thanks to me—someone who loves to travel—that he first considered tourism as a career. I have always had great interest in this region of the country, so it's very possible that my admiration and excitement renewed his strong feelings about his native land. The prospect of expressing his heartfelt love for the place, and extending his genuine sense of hospitality, may have influenced him, along with the realization that tourism could generate income for the people while preserving the region's many natural resources. Of course, I was never the kind of traveler who generated any income for them (on the contrary, they spent a lot of money on me), but I think I helped inspire them.

Chodrak said he was the lowest official among the low-ranking officials. Even so, arranging for horses to be brought from town for us wasn't a problem. Well, there was a slight problem. Usually, Chodrak could just give orders over the phone to have horses sent. However, my visit to Nyakchuka coincided with the season for a local activity even more lucrative than tourism—gathering *beshing shamo*, Matsutake mushrooms. When I arrived, none of the village's government workers were at their posts. One by one they had all run off to look for mushrooms. Not a single official in the village was answering his phone. Chodrak threw up his hands and had no choice but to dispatch one of his staff on horseback to carry his message.

This turned out to be effective. Apparently, in rural Tibetan areas, things still work best the old-fashioned way.

Three workers promptly arrived with horses for us. In addition to the workers, the trip to Horra would include Chodrak, me, and an exemplary "teacher of the people" named Tenzin. But what kind of official work could Chodrak say our group would be doing out on the grasslands? Without hesitation, Chodrak announced that we would be conducting research into a monastery in the town. Tenzin added that the township had a small school that was incomplete and needed to be inspected. But why was I coming along? With my two cameras hanging around my neck, everyone always assumed that I was a "journalist," so without further questions I had a justification for being part of the group. In reality, of course, Chodrak and Tenzin were accompanying me to meet Tokden Rinchen.

I never thought the journey to meet Rinchen would be so tedious. I only gradually came to realize the difficulty after I had been riding for some time on the back of a big horse, my saddlebags overstuffed with all kinds of junk. (I should mention that this junk included my backpack, which contained my sleeping bag, tape recorder and rolls of tape, film, my makeup and toiletries, and so forth. The other things in the saddlebags were quilts and overcoats, which were the only personal items that Chodrak and Tenzin took on the trip.) Chodrak's and Tenzin's horses carried our food supplies and a rice cooker. (For the record, I want to mention that we bought all these things ourselves and did not use any public funds; Chodrak and his colleagues never wanted to create the appearance that they were sponging off the people's money.)

We were riding our horses through a place where flowers were in full bloom, when Chodrak and Tenzin stopped. Saying they were "going to look for mushrooms," they left me with Tashi, the horse keeper, and disappeared into the woods. Tashi took the horses to graze nearby, and I lay down among the flowers. Against the meadow of wild grasses, the colorful flowers created the appearance of a brightly woven rug. I had the urge to burst into song in praise of Kham's amazing beauty. I had never felt such a strong urge to sing—and have never felt that way since. Unfortunately, I didn't know any songs capable of expressing the splendor around me. On top of that, even if I had thought of an appropriate song, my voice isn't good enough. I could not have done justice to either the song or the scenery. I realized that I was a Tibetan who had been estranged from the natural landscape for too long. Tashi, on the other hand, simply burst into song, and I couldn't get enough of his singing. What a wonderful voice he had.

When we were all riding together and Tashi wasn't singing, I liked listening to my taped music. I slipped my sore feet out of the stirrups and let them dangle alongside the horse's belly. Because I didn't feel like talking, I deliberately rode behind everyone else. I just enjoyed listening through my earphones to the slow chanting of an old lama who had been a hermit for many years, and the gentle rocking of the horse. Wherever I looked, the land was gorgeous. Then out of the blue, the horses started getting jittery, raising their heads and looking from side to side. I leaned low and caught sight of a slender snake swiftly disappearing into the grass. But I didn't see very much of anything before I was thrown off my horse and hit my head on a rock. My companions, riding in front, heard me shriek. They turned and hurriedly galloped back. In my head was the chanting of the lama's soft mantra, but it couldn't lessen the pain of hitting the ground. I immediately began to cry . . .

(Hey, hold on! I can't get offtrack and start talking about myself. I'm writing about Rinchen!)

Only after we had ridden over several mountains, crossed several rivers, and at last reached the Horra County government office (where we slept on the floor) did we finally meet Rinchen, the sky-burial master. People say his home pastures are very far from the county office, so when we arrived, Chodrak once again had to send messengers on horseback. When I first saw Rinchen, his brow was beaded with sweat, and his hands held the reins of an exhausted horse he was pulling along behind him. He had been tending to a sick cow and had been in the middle of giving it an injection when he received our message. He had immediately gotten on his horse and ridden fast for over six hours. I felt a bit ashamed. After all, he wasn't the one who had wanted to meet. How could I rudely bother him in this manner?

But Rinchen's face lit up with joy when he saw Chodrak, as though he was seeing his own son. They had known each other for years and had a firm friendship. Chodrak not only drank the tea Rinchen made but also ate his yogurt. Whenever Rinchen had to take part in a county livestock protection meeting away from Horra, he would stay in Chodrak's home. Such companionship was unusual. As head of the livestock protection department, Rinchen held the rank of a government official, but he was still widely regarded as a *tokden*. It's true that people depend on the *tokden* to be there after they die, but while they're alive, they more or less avoid him. *Tokdens* have a strange air about them, but Chodrak was a close friend nonetheless.

I was still puzzling over Rinchen's odor as he stood before me with his long, curly black hair and weather-beaten face. His thick body was bundled up in a military-green overcoat, his feet were squeezed into felt boots, and he walked with a limp, like many nomads who ride horses from the time they are very young. Almost sixty years old, he remarked that pretty soon he himself would need a *tokden*.

As we mounted up and headed toward the sky-burial ground, I once again let my horse trail the others. Up ahead, Rinchen and Chodrak were laughing and joking. In the distance I could see the sky-burial ground and could smell its unusual odor on the light breeze. In truth, it was the scent of death. When we were right on it, the sky-burial ground looked rather much like the surrounding quiet grassland. When you looked carefully, however, you could see the bloodstains spattered here and there, and notice where the grass seemed flattened and thin. There was also an abundance of insects.

We dismounted at a spot where the scent of death was strongest, and Rinchen's demeanor suddenly changed. He became very professional . . .

"Let me start by talking about the geomancy of the sky-burial site," he said. "This area wasn't just selected at random; a long time ago it was chosen by a lama. Take a good look at the site. Do you see how it resembles a raft? It's in fact a sort of raft. All kinds of corpses are brought here: male, female, old, young. Some are also monks. Mostly they are carried from the surrounding villages. But there is a limit to the number of corpses that can be brought to this sky-burial ground. If there are too many corpses, ghosts will appear. Like a raft, a sky-burial site can't hold everyone. I don't know how many years this site has been in use, only that it's been here for a long time. I've been a *tokden* for over twenty years now, and I've used the knife on over two hundred dead people. How many passed through here before I came? When I look around, I don't see enough space for too many more."

Rinchen took me by the arm, pointed to the grass under our feet, and squinted his eyes, as though he were trying to get me to look at all the dead people around us. But how could I be expected to see them? I became flustered and rose up on my tiptoes.

"If the dead are not given a good sky burial, they can become like the very scary ghosts painted in traditional murals: skeletons hovering over burial sites. I've never seen ghosts, but maybe the scent of death is so much on me that even the ghosts are repelled. In any case, plenty of other people have seen ghosts. Recently a young herder girl saw them.

"Unless they have died a violent death, most people here are given a sky burial. Others are sent to Horlung for sky burial. The burial site there is located on a hillside and is very big. All Lithang County's dead are sent there, so it attracts many flesh-eating vultures. The *tokden* there has only been

doing the work for ten years, but has already helped over 160 people pass through. He was my apprentice. The head lama is Tenzin Delek Rinpoche.[3]

"Cutting people up for burial takes practice; it cannot be done in an arbitrary way," Rinchen continued, squatting on the ground beside me. With a knife, he made a few scratches on a blue-green stone. The scratches represented a twisted human body and looked very lifelike. "First you have to cut the back, then you have to cut twice along the ribs, then you have to turn the body over and cut twice along the stomach. It's not done exactly the same way for everyone. For example, it's different with big people. For men, you have to cut at an angle, like this. For women, you have to cut vertically, and for monks, you have to cut according to the type of robe . . ."

While Rinchen was talking, I was taking a lot of pictures. Suddenly he asked me to take a photograph of him lying on the grass with his eyes closed

and his arms and legs twisted in different directions. "Everyone who is sent to the sky-burial site starts off looking something like this," he said. "I want to see what I'll look like after I'm brought here, after I'm dead. Please don't forget," Rinchen said very seriously. "You must send me the photos." Of course I promised that I would.

Standing up and pointing to the mountains in the distance, he said, "A few days ago, people were disputing over boundaries on the grassland and a person was killed. If you'd arrived a few days earlier, you could have seen how I cut that person. A huge number of vultures were flying around."

Actually, I had seen a sky burial before. Or, to be more precise, I had seen what could be called a sky burial, but it wasn't for a human being. In 1998, I had gone with a TV production team from Taiwan to see Tsurphu Monastery,[4] located in Toelung Dechen County, near Lhasa. During our stay, we paid a special visit to the monastery's sky-burial site.

The production team wanted to film the burial process, but human corpses aren't sent to the site every day. They therefore bought a cow's leg to use as a substitute. One of the monks took off his coat and wrapped the limb so that it resembled a human torso. After they placed it on the site and surrounded it with stones, two monks began burning incense and spreading tsampa and barley grain on the ground. Facing the sacred mountain, the sky-burial master sat beside the "corpse," began playing a drum and horn, and recited the Buddhist scriptures that call vultures to the sky burial. At this point, large carnivorous birds began to circle high overhead. We could hear a deep, haunting sound that made us shiver. The monk explained that you could identify the vultures by their white armpit feathers; the others were either eagles or large crows. He said that over a hundred vultures inhabited the holy mountain. Tantric Buddhism considers vultures to be the fiercest category of *dakinis*—embodiments of cosmic female energy—known as *shasa khandro*: breath-takers, flesh-eaters, blood-drinkers, and bone-chewers.

The winds picked up and the Tsurphu River was rushing at great speed. High above, the slowly circling vultures looked graceful, calm, and gentle, yet somehow arrogant. The leading edges of their enormous wings appeared gray and white; the broad part of their wings, all the way to the tips, was black. As the birds descended in a spiral, maneuvering in the wind, their trailing wing feathers spread open, like huge scissors. I was overwhelmed by such magnificence.

When the sky-burial master had thoroughly chopped up the meat with his knife and smashed the bones with rocks, the vultures, one by one, gradually landed on the ground nearby. They tucked their wings in and looked almost comical as they staggered forward on legs and feet that seemed too skinny to support their thick bodies. (They reminded me of the way Rinchen walks.) The master threw pieces of meat to them, but they were in no rush to eat. They encircled the meat, hunched over with their heads down, and hissed. The master began talking to them in a warm, gentle voice, as if the vultures were his friends. A monk explained to us that the sky-burial master was inviting the "boss" of the vultures to take the first bite. Until the "boss" ate, the rest of the vultures would stay back. The master knew nearly every vulture by name, according to the monk. Presently, a particularly ferocious-looking vulture slowly stepped out of the crowd of birds and started to eat. Immediately, the rest rushed in and pushed each other out of the way to get their share. I heard the sky-burial master saying, "Hey! Do not fight; there is enough for all of you."

More and more vultures landed, hissing and making their strange noises. I counted about eighty. "It's quite rare to see so many vultures," the sky-burial master told me excitedly. "Sometimes only a few come, even if a human corpse is here." When that happens, the sky-burial master explained, it is because the person had committed so many sins—the vultures considered the corpse too dirty to eat. When a lot of vultures show up and won't eat the corpse, it is because the family of the dead person failed to perform the religious funeral rites. Today was quite unique, a monk said, because they had asked His Holiness Karma Kuchen Rinpoche for special permission and instructions. This sky burial had thus received His Holiness's blessings and empowerment.

The sky-burial master, a former monk of Tsurphu Monastery, was over sixty years old. When I asked him about his occupation, he said that he was continually inspired by the story of Buddha compassionately feeding his own body to the hungry tiger. The master imagined he was each corpse as he chopped it up and fed it to the *shasa khandro dakinis* of the Ten Directions. In that way, he said, he believed his occupation was sacred.

What about Rinchen—how did he become a *tokden*? (Having gotten off-track with so many digressions, I'm finally turning to this important question.) Rinchen told me, "Originally, I was a nomad, like all my ancestors on the Horra grasslands. I considered becoming a monk, but when 'democratic reforms' started, the Party working group tried to turn me into a revolutionary cadre. They saw, though, that I was too softhearted and couldn't help being concerned about the horses and cows whenever they got sick or injured. So I became a veterinarian, because the revolution also needed vets.

"One thing the revolution did not need was *tokden*. For quite a long time, sky burials were banned here, since the practice was considered to be among the 'Four Olds' that the Cultural Revolution wanted to destroy.[5] As a result, the dead were either buried in the ground or secretly thrown into rivers. For the families of the deceased, nothing could have been worse: The souls of those who did not go through the sky-burial ceremony could not escape from purgatory, and most probably became ghosts. After the Cultural Revolution, Tenzin Delek Rinpoche said to me, 'I noticed that you're very kind to the livestock; you even suck their wounds. This means you possess compassion for the dead as well and are highly suitable to be a *tokden*.' By this time, I'd joined the Communist Party. It'd never occurred to me that a Party member could become a *tokden*. But without a *tokden*, people were suffering an unsafe and uneasy death, which is a horrible thing. In addition, the most popular Communist Party slogan is 'Serve the People,' and to be a *tokden* is serving the people."

It was surprising to see how Rinchen had put Chairman Mao's guidance into practice. I praised him by saying, "Rinchen, across all of China—no, across the whole world—you are the only member of the Communist Party who is a *tokden*." And then I changed my tone and asked sternly, "Do you receive any payment?"

Rinchen flashed his snow-white teeth at me as if in ridicule, but with goodwill. By this time, we had reached the Horra township government building and dismounted. The setting sun had turned the mountains behind the sky-burial site a golden yellow. The beauty was stunning and incomparable. Rinchen went into his office and came back with a large sheet of white paper. He drew two columns on the paper, then began to fill them in with names followed by numbers. What did it mean?

Rinchen explained, "This is a list of all the dead persons for whom I performed sky burial. These are their names, and in this column are the amounts of money their families offered me. The families themselves decided the amounts: five yuan, ten yuan, twenty yuan, up to fifty yuan. It's fine with me if they don't have any money: I just put down a zero. But why have I drawn this list? It's because I want to show that I remember these people. I do not spend any of this money on myself. I have enough in salary, a little over two hundred yuan. I give some of these payments to the poor, and the rest goes to repairing places used for prayer."

How interesting. Judging by the way he kept records, it was obvious that Rinchen was a responsible civil servant. A common nomad would have kept records by tying knots or using some other primitive method. I was deeply moved by the way Rinchen practiced his unique profession.

At that point, Tenzin called us in for dinner. He had stayed at the county government office to cook for us. I was pleasantly surprised that he had not only fried shredded potatoes, but also cooked mushrooms that he and Chodrak had found, mixing these with canned braised pork. It was such a delicious meal.

Despite the peculiar smell that lingered on his body, Rinchen joined us for dinner. We were able to ignore it even though the room in the building was quite small. It was sparsely furnished, with a shaky table, four rickety

wooden stools, and a steel stove for heating tea and cooking. Firewood was scattered all over the floor. Oh, yes: There was also an old, yellow, rotary-dial phone on the table. The space served as the government meeting room for the township. It couldn't be called just the township's office because it was also the meeting space for the Women's Federation, Youth League Committee, Office of Family Planning, and People's Armed Forces Division. However, no one from these groups was around, and all business was closed. As I mentioned earlier, all the civil servants had gone to look for mushrooms. Outside, some monks in robes were playing basketball. They were from the nearby monastery and had been asked to temporarily take care of the routine government matters. I noticed that they were carrying the keys to several offices, so I teased them by asking, "Isn't this the same as seizing power?"

Of course there was at least one civil servant on duty. His name was Kelsang Gonpo. I can't recall what his title was, but I still remember his distinct appearance and manner. He had messy curly hair, a dark complexion, and eyes as big as a yak's, which were red from drinking. Chodrak said harshly to him, when he entered the room, "You're a complete alcoholic!" Paying no attention, Kelsang Gonpo roughly dialed the rotary phone. Supposedly, dialing this phone would make all the telephones in the four nearby townships ring. But the switchboard was closed. To my amazement, he eventually managed to make this outdated communication device work, reaching a township leader who had just returned from looking for mushrooms. In his weird Chinese, Kelsang Gonpo shouted into the telephone, "Whether you come back soon or not, people are on the verge of being killed over here! Whether you come back or not, we have no power to settle their disagreements!" It turned out that the government recently had been redrawing the border between Nyakchuka and Lithang Counties, triggering territorial disputes among nomads from both counties. Apparently over fifty nomads from Yonru, Lithang, had banded together and were determined to take back their traditional grasslands, which had been allocated to other people when the borders were redrawn. Dissatisfaction was escalating among nomads in nearby places.

A heated discussion on the important subject of boundary settlements was soon underway in that small room. Disputes over grassland boundaries were never-ending in the Tibetan nomadic areas. Almost every year, disputes among townships, counties, regions, and prefectures grew so intense that lives were lost. The primary cause of the grassland disputes began in the 1950s, when Tibetan areas were divided into several new administrative regions. Now, after a series of failures, all levels of government had run out of ideas for dealing with the problem. Even if soldiers were dispatched, it made no difference. The only effective solutions came about when disputes were handled by a person highly respected by everyone, such as Tenzin Delek Rinpoche, who had settled conflicts a number of times. But let me stop my digression here and return to discussing Rinchen.

It started raining heavily, and rolling thunder boomed through the darkness. Lightning struck the telephone line hanging through the window, creating a burst of dazzling sparks. Screaming as though his hair had been set on fire, Kelsang Gonpo ran from the room. I lit candles that I had brought and continued listening to Rinchen's story. The lightning seemed to have ignited some deep, suppressed passion in him. His whole body became animated. Words and expressions in his native Nyuchangwa came rushing out.[6] The sound of Rinchen's Nyuchangwa overlapped with more thunder and the voices of Chodrak and Tenzin as they tried simultaneously to act as interpreters. All that's now on my tape recorder is a jumble of noise, so I'm unable to retrieve Tokden Rinchen's fascinating expressions. What a great shame. However, I did take down the following sentences:

Life is short and uncertain. Today you see this person herding yaks; tomorrow he may be sent for sky burial. So I too do not know when I'll be eaten by the vultures. Maybe I'll still be here in ten years, or maybe I'll die in a few days. Every time I cut a corpse, I think of myself as the dead person, and I pray that I'll have a good reincarnation for the next life . . . Whether diagnosing livestock or cutting a corpse, I was in the habit of eating tsampa without washing my hands, even though they were often covered in blood. I do not think of the blood as dirty. I believe the blood from other lives is the same as my own blood. One day, however, Tenzin Delek Rinpoche told me that while it was good that I cared for animals just as I cared for human beings, it's not good to eat blood, which may carry viruses and affect my next life. Since then, I've abandoned my bad habit and now clean my hands before every meal.

Chodrak and Tenzin went outside to the toilet, and I was left alone listening to Rinchen, who continued speaking passionately. A sudden explosion of thunder and lightning blew out all the candles except one. In the dim, flickering light of the remaining candle, Rinchen's facial expressions changed constantly. They made me imagine all the dead people he had performed sky burial for. I became so terrified that I was about to run out when my two "bodyguards" came back.

The next day was sunny, without a trace of the heavy rain from the night before. The Horra grasslands were as exquisite as a lotus that has emerged from the water. Early in the morning, Rinchen came to say goodbye: Four calves had died, and he had to go vaccinate the others. He held my hands for a long time. The peculiar smell still emanated from his body, but I was at ease with it. I now know why he was so kind and friendly to me. It is because I came from Lhasa, the holiest place for him. He gave me one hundred yuan and asked me to light butter lamps when I returned to Lhasa and to pray for the dead in front of Jokhang Temple. He said to me sadly—and it saddened me too—"If I'm still alive in a few years, I'll make a pilgrimage to Lhasa. I really want to visit the Jokhang Temple and see Jowo Rinpoche."[7]

As Rinchen mounted his horse and set off, I watched him gradually disappear into the distance. Although it could be said he had several identities, I understood that deep down he was, after all, a typical nomad. History had bestowed on him a unique identity, but that identity seemed to me redundant now, and vanishing without a trace. It was futile to expect that I could have found in him the identity that I had sought in the beginning. Somehow this made me feel sad, but also relieved. It is precisely the pluralism of their identities that turns a great many Tibetans into two, three persons, sometimes even more. What I mean is that I have seen many Tibetans with divided hearts and personalities. For instance, I know elderly people who have been given the identity "retired civil servant," and who lead meaningless lives with no sense of belonging. Of course this is a complicated topic. So I can only say that on this seemingly unchanging—and yet seemingly ever-changing—Horra grassland, Rinchen is simply Rinchen.

Two years later, I returned to Nyakchuka, but I did not see Rinchen. Chodrak said he was still alive but was no longer a *tokden*. A year after that, I went to Nyakchuka once again, and Chodrak invited me for dinner. Unexpectedly, there at the dining table sat Rinchen, smiling at me. He appeared much older, and when he smiled, I saw he had lost many teeth. When he was not smiling, the depth of his eye sockets and the thinness of his face made his head seem like a skull. I noticed the old smell was no longer on his body. With a look of great satisfaction, he told me that his lifelong wish had finally been fulfilled: He had been to Lhasa and seen Jowo Rinpoche. He then said that he had planned to visit me in Lhasa, but was unaware that the city was so big and crowded. He had stood in the temple and shouted my name, but to no avail. He told me he had received the photographs I had taken of him, and sure enough, he looked exactly like the corpses waiting for sky burial.

April 4, 2004—Beijing

NOTES

1. *Tokden* is Tibetan for "sky-burial master." [author's note]

2. *Renminbi*, or RMB, is the yuan, the Chinese currency.

3. In April 2002, three years following the conversation described in this piece, Tenzin Delek Rinpoche, a widely revered reincarnated lama, was arrested and tortured. Convicted by the Chinese government of "inciting splittism," he was sentenced to death. After international appeals on his behalf, in 2005 his sentence was commuted to life imprisonment. Tenzin Delek Rinpoche died in detention in July 2015, prompting an international outcry.

4. The main monastery of the Karma Kagyu lineage of Tibetan Buddhism.

5. The "Four Olds" are "Old Customs, Old Culture, Old Habits, and Old Ideas."

6. "Nyuchangwa" is the local Chinese term used for the nomads.

7. In Sanskrit: Shakyamuni. [author's note]

5

Tibet

When I saw him he was already gone. Right here.
From here to there, strands of long hair
        entangled. Like sutra streamers.
A beam of light flares, stronger. And dies.
Snow melts.
Are my knees hurting?
I'd rather stay silent between *khatas*,[1]
        but narrate with empty hands.
Over these centuries, there's always a silent man, a good soul.
Which round of tap dance has chosen your feet?
See how black and white governs their eyes, melts in the sun.
Spirit above matter.
Lotus, nectar, and rainbow on the pilgrim road.
Just one step. You're no longer where you were.
Mountain is mountain. Water is water. Who eats yak butter and tsampa?

> *Once I find an ideal place,*
> *I want to build my tent.*
> *But the rope breaks,*
> *how can I not feel sad!*

Snow melts very slowly, but why the need to race for time.
No one values his treasure at home, regrets when it falls into foreign hands.
Incense is still burning today.
        Burning over today.
Guess, what should they do when they can't find their gods?
Sing to your heart. Dance to your heart.
        How many more cycles of reincarnation do you need?
We die of small wounds but are resurrected.
Like a spider spinning its web to the voices of sutra.
What a simple view.

What a rich mind.
A horse takes you to the destination.

> *Horses have run away from the pastures,*
> *half of them gone.*
> *Not the horses,*
> *but the riders' hearts gone.*

Everyone turns round and round. Like rising in specks.
Where is the way? The way isn't at your feet.
       Of course there are cars, planes. Or trains.
When I suddenly turn back, he's gone.
I prosper from selling a skull cup and nine-eye stones.
I bring ordinary men into his garden.
All will disperse when all ends. When will he return?
I found a small brass spoon in a village.
       (Rumors say witches used it to scoop up water, wine, homemade
       soup five centuries ago.)
There is a Chinese saying, *A blessing or a curse in disguise.* Let alone money.
This is why I die like a dog. And live like a dog now.
One day at a time.
Such glaring sun. Such a dark sky.
Let's sleep.
People arrive in our sleep.
Those who must sleep will always sleep. Law will always be maintained.
   How about those who mustn't sleep?
Some will leave with the rich.
       Some just follow others until death.
Tears pour.

Never forget how your hat and shoes look when they can't find you.
Even words floating in the air can cast blue shadows . . .

You look quite lovely in Tibetan clothes. The banner too.
Green barley is no longer good for brewing beer.
Still we praise its taste.
Tibetan wine, my home wine.
     Om mani padme hum.
If it's fun here, we'll settle down. We'll drink any tea that tastes sweet.

Just run your own course.
Damn! Why're you pregnant again?
Leaves are falling.
How about a musical instrument for her to try?
His deformed face is full of tears.
Wake up, wake up, says the child.
I know him.
The day he was born, petals rained from the sky. Birds landed on branches.
A halo shines in his left palm.
He is now a freshman in a Tibetan high school in Beijing.
O snow, must you melt so slowly?
They have been waiting for good weather to no avail.
Only I remain now: neither fish nor fowl.

> *The swamp west of Lhasa was once an execution site,*
> *now ghostly at night.*
> *O, I love most the Han language I know.*
> *But where are my rosaries?*

The man with a deformed head is still weeping,
but who cares.
We can't even retrieve a single strand of hair from this land. So let's dream.

   December 1990, Lhasa

NOTE

   1. *Khatas* are traditional ceremonial scarves in Tibetan culture.

6

Garpon La's Offerings

I didn't know him personally, but I've heard many stories about Garpon La. There are even more that I haven't heard, and in fact some people emphatically and even angrily say that the Garpon La I've heard stories about isn't the one who went to Dharamsala; and the Garpon La who did go to Dharamsala isn't the same Garpon La I've heard about. This sounds a bit like a brain teaser. It's enough to make you dizzy.

Added to this is the fact that I'm using the honorific term *La* to refer to the person whose story I want to tell, though I don't actually know if I should, and the question doesn't really matter to me anyway. Honestly, I am not even that interested in sorting out one Garpon La from another. This is probably a mistake. By not doing much research, I have to rely on my memory. However, while obstacles I've created for myself are troubling, I don't intend to talk about Garpon La's life and achievements anyway; they aren't important. What I mean to say is that they're not important to this story. After all, I'm not writing his biography; I want to relate just one incident.

I should also say that these events occurred during a confusing time. That doesn't mean I've forgotten things, but it's possible the story has become muddled. I've told and retold it on ten or more occasions. Every time I tell it, the regret that weighs on my heart becomes heavier.

I remember the bright, summer-afternoon sunshine two years ago, and the homey atmosphere of a certain Tibetan restaurant in Unity Village. Flowers in full bloom lined the windows, and through them I could see people outside playing music on the Tibetan lute *dramnyen* and singing "Chadey Karpo [White Bird]." They played very loudly, which at first doesn't seem to fit this nostalgic scene, but that's all right. Garpon La's disciples were robust, and their big voices clanged like a huge bell, just the way slow, Garlu music is

supposed to sound.[1] At that time, Garpon La was no longer young: His hair was graying, and he had retired. Thinking of him now, I feel regret because I promised him I would write down the stories he told me about incidents in Lhasa. But I've procrastinated until many of the stories seem like floating clouds at the end of the world, gradually fading into a mist.

Not so long ago, a dusty book fell from my bookshelf and practically landed in my hands. I took it as a sign, and decided that, no matter what, I must finally write down this story. That book was crudely manufactured, with no serial number or publisher's markings except for one line, in Chinese, on the back: PRINTED BY TIBET XINHUA PUBLISHING HOUSE. Everything else was in Tibetan. The cover had been designed using Tibetan colors and patterns, which, like the Tibetan script, appeared to be dancing. Because of the story I'm about to tell, I now recognize that the eight-petal, red-and-blue lotus flowers on the book's cover are bunched together to represent a *damma* drum. And below the figure of the eight auspicious signs and what looks like clouds are two Tibetan oboes, *suna*. The *damma* drum and *suna* were brought to Tibet a long time ago and used in court song and dance performances known as Gar. Titled *Songs and Dances for Offerings*, the book contained musical scores and lyrics for fifty-eight Gar performances.

Published in January 1985, *Songs and Dances for Offerings* had been in my father's collection of Tibetan books. He had served in the army all his life—as

would be expected, given the period in which he lived—and he loved Tibetan revolutionary songs in the style of *toeshey*, *gorshey*, and *nangma*, as well as Gar and all popular folk and love songs from Ü-Tsang Province. Among his books were numerous musical journals, all of which still exhaled the atmosphere of the times. I brought all of them to Beijing with me, where they took up over a meter's worth of space on my bookshelf. *Songs and Dances for Offerings* was one of the volumes I hadn't gotten around to browsing.

As soon as I opened the book, I was enormously excited to see a photograph of Garpon La. Yes, it really was Garpon La, sitting on a simple chair and holding a *suna* in his hands. Behind his glasses, his eyes looked old and somewhat anxious. From the surroundings, I could tell that the photograph

ད་ལྟ་སྐུ་ཕྱིང་…
བཙ་བཞིན་……
དུས་ཀྱི་གར་…
མཁན་འདགའ་"
གུས་དང་རོལ་
ཆ་སོགས་རོ་…
སྤྲད།

was taken in the People's Stadium of Lhasa. Situated near the banks of the Kyichu River, the area had once been verdant and lush. Since the 1950s, it became the place where tens of thousands of people gathered for political assemblies to celebrate the Cultural Revolution, for instance, which was then sweeping through Lhasa. It was also the place for big demonstrations denouncing the American imperialist invasion of Vietnam, and for the noisy public trials of "antirevolutionary elements," people who were counterrevolutionary criminals.

Of course, in the photograph the stadium was silent. The grounds were empty and overgrown with weeds. Garpon La appeared to be sitting alone. He was smiling in an elegant, very Lhasa way that belonged to the Lhasa of times past. I could tell it was a smile from Lhasa's past, even though the photograph was taken before I was born: It expressed an old-fashioned, illusory gaiety. The impression of times past was perhaps emphasized by the ornate clothing Garpon La was wearing: the flat, round cap, the long earring dangling from his left ear, the golden-yellow brocade gown over a pure-white collar and sleeves, and the red boots with blue soles. The clothing had been specially made, but when I first saw the photograph, I knew nothing about the reasons he was dressed in such a way. For example, it appeared to me that he was wearing the gold-and-turquoise earrings called *sochen*, even though such jewelry was only worn by aristocrats, high officials, and occasionally by wealthy businessmen. His outfit seemed to come from a time long before the 1980s—when the photograph was taken—and of course from long before 2009, when I first saw it. Nevertheless, Garpon La looked stunning beyond compare—an impression that is hard to describe. Behind him on the rostrum, bulky blood-red pillars had been pushed together. They struck me as rude and inappropriate. I felt them stabbing at my eyes, and I was suddenly overcome by sorrow.

Even a short introduction in a book can reveal a lot of information. This was the case with *Songs and Dances for Offerings*, with its brief introduction to the Fourteenth Dalai Lama's eleven-member dance troupe. After a few pages, only bits of information about the troupe emerged, such as the number of members and their ages. There wasn't a lot, but at the time it probably wasn't safe to write much more. The introduction seemed to be quite ordinary, even mediocre. Nevertheless, much information was hidden between the lines. These nuances could only be understood by another Tibetan, who would discern from just a glance what was really being said, what happened when and where. Many Tibetan readers experienced the hardship and torment the troupe endured before they had at last survived the disasters in their lives. Anyone who hasn't experienced similar torments will find it hard to read between the lines of the writing and know what the men went through. That's why a narrator like me is needed, who is at some distance from the incidents but is sympathetic to their reality and able to retell the story. I must say, though, that the only reason I am able to enter, even temporarily, the collective memory of these events is because of the help I've received from those who survived.

Take, for example, what the introduction says about Garpon Pasang Dhondup. He joined the Gar Song and Dance Troupe at age nine. At twenty-one, he served as a Gar musician, having mastered many instruments. At thirty-two, he became the head Gar musician and was given the title Garpon [Master]. At forty-three, he upheld the "Democratic Reforms." At that point, the introduction doesn't reveal that the year was 1959, or say what happened next. Twenty-two years of his life are omitted without comment. Suddenly the year is 1981, and we learn that Garpon Pasang Dhondup participated in the first TAR [Tibet Autonomous Region] Conference on Literatures and Arts, reintroducing Gar to the agenda. The section on him concludes by saying that at age sixty-four, in 1982, he was absorbed in saving the Gar tradition, whose transmission had almost come to an end.

So where was Garpon La during those twenty-two years? And what about the other members of the Gar Song and Dance Troupe? It seems as if each of them was also lost for twenty-two years, as if they had all evaporated, had disappeared without a trace. I don't know if the others in the troupe shared a similar experience, but according to what his students told me on that summer afternoon in Unity Village, Garpon La was arrested by the People's Liberation Army, charged with being an "insurgent," imprisoned, and later sent to the "reeducation through labor camp" in Gormo. Prisoners in that camp constructed railways and the Qinghai–Tibet Highway. But how many years was he there? How many other people were in the camp, and how long were their sentences? History becomes very murky here. Nobody seems to have any answer. We only know that Garpon La was among the very few who—old, weak, sick, and injured—came back from the Gormo labor camp alive.

Before going on, I should explain a little about what Gar is. As I mentioned earlier, Gar is a form of Tibetan court song and dance performance. Over four centuries ago, it came directly to the Tibetan court from the kingdom of Ladakh, when the Fifth Dalai Lama was enthroned. Gar was regarded thereafter as sacred music dedicated to the Dalai Lama and performed only during special, high ceremonies. According to the book *The Auspicious Banquet for Heart, Ear, and Eyes*, the most important score in Gar music is "Lucky, Happy, Plentiful." The lyrics go roughly like this:

> The vast beautiful empty sky of today overhead,
> the fortunate earth is happy,
> here is a lucky, happy, and plentiful time,
> beginning songs and dances of offering,
> dedicated to the enlightened sage,
> all-knowing ocean of wisdom,
> field of happiness, King of Dharma,
> respect and admiration for the sacred ruler.

Other important musical scores include "Sacred Land of Lhasa," "Rays of the Sun," "Reverent Prostrations," "Cloud Offering," and "Star in the Sky." The Gar court troupe consisted of thirteen boys chosen from very good backgrounds, who were trained from a young age with meticulous care. People from Lhasa speak of their having "an honorable and glorious obligation" because they performed for the Dalai Lama at all kinds of ceremonies, celebrations, and meetings. They praised the deities and Gongsachog [Dalai Lama] with sparkling, clear songs and regal dancing. Each artist wore beau-

tifully colored costumes resembling those worn by the celestial beings de-
picted in murals. Lhasa people said, "It's only those fortunate women who
can win the hearts of performers with Changdi clothes." Of course, they had
to wait until the pure children had been transformed by their training into
splendid and good-looking performing artists. When the boys reached the
age of eighteen, they would have to return to society and assume a role in
the secular world.

All that belonged to the Old Tibet, however. People in the New Tibet,
such as myself, have only seen song and dances performed by the Tibetan
opera troupe or by performers in *nangma*. Unfortunately, these performances are too embedded in secular values and influences to be pure. The
earliest *nangma* emerged around the 1990s. At the time, it was still worth
going to see them. Many old people performed traditional *toeshey*, *gorshey*,
and *nangma*, and those people in the audience were allowed to go on the
stage and dance. I've taken my mother and aunts to the *nangma* performed
today. My uncle, who trained as a dancer, came along with us once, exam-
ined everything with a critical eye, and said in a dissatisfied voice that things
had already changed for the worse. I wouldn't know what the real thing was
like, but it was still enchanting when my mother and aunts were gracefully
singing and dancing. It's true, though, that you don't need to be an expert
to see that today's *nangma* are simply a nauseating mixture of Chinese and
Tibetan pop music, performed by degenerate men and women—nothing

more. Fortunately, the *nangma* dances do not attempt to include Gar. Reduced to such circumstances, Gar would be an omen of catastrophe.

I now have to return to the Garpon La story. I'm always like this: I mean to say one thing, but then start going on about something else. It's really a bit embarrassing.

After Garpon Pasang Dhondup La survived the hellish Gormo labor camps, he returned to an unrecognizable Lhasa. The sight was terribly disheartening. At the time, the popular saying was *Many things waiting to be done.* This meant that the catastrophe was over; everything could start anew, including the recovery of things—such as Gar—that had been treated as "feudal superstition" and swept into the dustbin of history by the Cultural Revolution. However, even in the big city of Lhasa, Gar had disappeared. Feeling guilty, the Party and the government repeatedly asked Garpon La to come out of retirement and restore Gar. But he refused. People say that Garpon La pointed to the scars on his body and very politely said, "Sorry. Because the 'reeducation through labor' I received at Gormo was so thorough, I've completely forgotten Gar." Listening to him explain this again and again, with his scars looking ever more shocking, the Party and the government became too embarrassed to continue bothering him. Around this time, the Party and the government were trying to improve their image.

In the 1980s, the first official contacts began between Beijing and Dharamsala. Separated for twenty years, Tibetans inside and outside the country gained a little more freedom of movement. I don't know what brought luck to Garpon La, but when he applied for a passport that would permit him to visit relatives in Nepal or some other country, it was granted to him. I should note that India was not among the countries Tibetans were allowed to visit—a strict rule that continues today. Nevertheless, when Tibetans wish to travel abroad, their final destination is usually India—Dharamsala, in the northern part of India, to be exact. There is only one reason for wanting to go to Dharamsala: to meet the Dalai Lama. Actually, this is hardly any big secret.

Summarizing all the details, I'll just say that Garpon La eventually went to Dharamsala and saw Kundun [the Dalai Lama]. Coincidentally, that was Kundun's twenty-fourth year in exile, his *ka* year.[2] Garpon La was past middle age, and numerous times had dedicated splendid Gar to Kundun. With deep respect, he had watched the challenges that the God-King had faced during his life. And now he was in a foreign country where he hoped once again to see him; to Garpon La, there was no miracle more impermanent than meeting Kundun. My own Buddhist master used to tell me, "Suffering is impermanent, happiness is impermanent." What an honest and true saying.

Once he was before the Dalai Lama, Garpon La couldn't help bursting into tears. People say he sobbed and pleaded, "Kundun, please give permission to this troupe-of-one to make offerings to Kundun with Gar. For more than two decades, this body hasn't been used to express Gar. It's been waiting for this day to once more be used in a dedication to Kundun."

I don't know whether the Dalai Lama, during his long years of exile, was likely to have an appreciation for Gar, once called "delightful to the eye." After all, when the Dalai Lama departed Lhasa, the Gar troupe was shut down within days. What the Chinese could seize was seized, what could be shut down was shut down, what could be scattered was scattered. Had there been another Gar troupe that could follow Kundun into exile to Dharamsala? At this moment, the aging Garpon La—who for more than twenty years had been cut off from Gar—was alone, surrounded entirely by exiles. And yet he wanted to make traditional offerings to His Holiness.

People say that when Garpon La started tapping the *damma* drum and singing with his desolate voice, the sounds of crying and weeping filled the house, enclosing the air of a foreign country but smelling of the incense of Lhasa. And His Holiness also quietly shed tears. Afterward, people say, Garpon La announced, in effect, that by having dedicated Gar to Kundun for the final time, he had been granted the wish that kept him alive during his many years of hard labor. So from then on, he would only perform Gar songs in the heavens, even if it meant allowing Gar to disappear from the earth. He would rather risk the danger that Gar would become a lost tradition than perform Gar again in the secular world.

His Holiness closed his eyes slightly, seeming to quell the flood of his emotions. After remaining motionless for a while, he slowly began speaking. He said that he did not quite agree with Garpon La. Not only did he disagree, he also obligated Garpon La to return to Lhasa and to transform Gar into a ceremony for the public to see. "You have to perform again," Kundun said. "In fact, you will go back to Lhasa and accept the invitation of the Party and government to restore Gar. You will also recruit a number of Tibetan boys and teach them. You can make reforms by teaching Gar to Tibetan girls. In short, no matter the obstacles, you must not let Gar disappear."[3]

I've quoted His Holiness's statement to Garpon La as if I had been present at the scene. I did this in order to make the story more dramatic. In any event, according to Garpon La, he regarded what was said to him as a perfect teaching that effectively changed his life. When he returned to Lhasa, it was like a miracle. Almost overnight, the entire city knew what had happened:

that unexpectedly the nearly forgotten Gar had been recalled into existence; that Gar, once banished like Garpon La, was returning to Lhasa. This news was a source of joy and made Garpon La so happy that he let bygones be bygones. The stigma of "insurgent," given to him by the Party, was washed from his records. He received awards and became a famous court musician. As a celebrated expert in Gar, he was also given the title "Professor of Music" by Tibet University. How dramatic all this was! Having suffered torment for so long, in his final years he radiated with glory in the brilliance of "New Tibet."

People say it was as though a tree made of iron had suddenly blossomed with flowers, as though a mute had begun to speak, when Garpon La gathered his troupe in front of the Party's cultural officials and began to beat the *damma* drum. That voice of desolation sang without hurry:

> Beginning songs and dances of offering,
> dedicated to the enlightened sage,
> all-knowing ocean of wisdom,
> field of happiness, King of Dharma,
> respect and admiration for the sacred ruler.

I'm absolutely certain that nobody in the audience had ears in the least bit qualified to listen respectfully to Gar. During the previous decades, their ears became tarnished, stuffed with earwax. How could they appreciate this devotional, beautiful, splendid music of compassion, of *nying-je*?[4] Consequently, Garpon La turned his gaze inward, into the center of the void, as though he hoped to see the Dharamsala in his mind, where Kundun would be nodding his head and smiling, intoxicated by the spiritual music coming from Lhasa. Garpon La couldn't help shedding tears.

Music from suffering, the true meaning of impermanence in dharma, was once again heard in the world. No doubt Garpon La had mixed feelings. He became more meticulous and devoted to his work. In the last years of his life, on the eve of leaving this world and rushing toward rebirth, he turned to modern science and technology. He recorded dozens of Gar songs on CDs, which could be reproduced countless times. Heavenly music for the benefit of all sentient beings, including me, a lost sheep. Nowadays, having transferred all these Gar songs to my iPhone, I can listen to them whenever and wherever I want. Sacred Gar music has joined a myriad of other songs, to last forever in the secular world. For this reason, I want to pay tribute to Garpon La. Because of Gar, he may have already been reincarnated into a deity, his thousand arms extended, and a thousand bright eyes looking over

Chenrezig's pure earth as he continues to make his indescribably beautiful offerings.[5] *Kunchok Sum!*[6]

Summer 2009, Lhasa
Revised—July 2016, Beijing

NOTES

1. Garlu is Gar music composed for the Dalai Lama.

2. Tibetans believe that every twelve years, starting from a person's birth, one is prone to bad luck. This is called a *ka* year. The Dalai Lama was born in 1935, so when Garpon La arrives in Dharamsala in 1983, it is a *ka* year for the Dalai Lama, which makes their meeting perilous.

3. Traditionally, women could not be taught Gar, just as women in Mongolia were not allowed to learn *khoomei* (throat-singing). By insisting that Gar be taught to girls, His Holiness was acknowledging that the Tibetan culture was facing an imminent crisis that had to be avoided.

4. According to His Holiness the Dalai Lama, *nying-je*'s meanings include "love, affection, kindness, gentleness, generosity of spirit, and warm-heartedness ... [It also] denotes a feeling of connection with others, reflecting its origin in empathy, and is both the source and the result of patience, tolerance, forgiveness, and all good qualities." See the chapter "*Nying-je*, the Supreme Emotion" in the Dalai Lama's *Ancient Wisdom, Modern World: Ethics for a New Millennium* (London: Abacus/Little, Brown, 1999). [Abacus is an imprint of Little, Brown]

5. Chenrezig is the Buddha of Compassion. [author's note]

6. Literally, this means the three Precious Jewels of Buddhism (the Buddha, the Dharma, and the Sangha). It is also used as an expression roughly equivalent to "On the three Precious Jewels, I swear this is true" or "By the three Precious Jewels, may this be so." [author's note]

7

On the Fifteenth Midnight
of the Fourth Month
in the Tibetan Calendar

So a stainless Dolma
from top to bottom, blends into the crowd
Too much compassion has transformed her
A girl with no need to look lovely
holds my hand
with light from yesterday
and speaks tirelessly of karma

Flocks of vultures
like voices of mediums
disperse body and soul
let eastern purple clouds guide the way
A voice from somewhere
simple, allusive
saves every child prodigy lost to the profane

But here, in the rising Tibet
where divinity nourishes daylight
petty ghosts return
against heterodoxy
Secretly they count themselves lucky
Urged by irresistible illusions
they can't afford to lose

Only this mystical Dolma
walks behind
pitying these men—
by chance in a glance at some handprint
a life hesitates and wanders
between the gifted and the common

When the sun shines, she too disappears
in all emptiness[1]

June 1991, Lhasa

NOTE

1. The fifteenth day of the fourth month in the Tibetan calendar is the day of the Buddha's birth, enlightenment, and passing on. It is known as "Saga Dawa" in Tibetan. [author's note]

8

The Prayer Beads of Fate

Two Excerpts

Late at night, she observes
all suppressed emotions
surging from fingertips to the edge of a sky
Ever-changing clouds and colors
as unfathomable as her life
Should she summon back
those radiant men?

How do those who seem to be of this world
manage to live peacefully
in huts full of pure sounds
their only home?
An only kin
is a tragic figure
Yet she feels useless
often hurt
chagrined

Such a rare crowd
naive and pure
ringing their bells
on a dark red path
Have they seen a rainbow
with Heaven on the other end?
Jade stones sparkle, lotus blossom
Please bestow sympathy
in red dust
under a gaudy umbrella
The girl who weeps for love
is a jade bowl almost filled to its brim
spilling

not a drop of wine

Dark night of Tibet!
Stars like promises
gradually reveal the heart
Weariness wearier than weariness
what else can she express?
If she must travel afar again
If she ages further

*

In a racially diverse province
a temporary destination
she sinks into the boisterous dusk
next, a massive blackness
like familiar faces
love in the time of cholera
like unrestrainable wine
or waves of secret sobs
fill the brain indistinctly

Only, only
those hundred and eight
ovals
in black
tied together by a knot with a yellow thread
She almost cries out
O, prayer beads!
but her hand quivers
splattering a cup of wine

Must be spring now
such pure dewdrops on new leaves
Only a blossoming young woman
can wear them on her cheeks
around her free neck
She has now aged too fast
in a foreign land, a foreign paper
running untimely
with a pride full of sorrow

These were once your precious
when you took a meandering
path, a kasaya
in clouds of red dust
alone but free
with glistening tears
and a hand ceaselessly twisting the beads
Have you already forgotten
what you can't let go?

Outside the monastery
pieces of paper waltz like desires
How arrogant!
To think of defeating a man who sighs before the sky

    1994, Lhasa

9

The King of *Dzi*

If you had ever met Karma, you would certainly not forget him.[1] Karma is a man whose physique and aura are hard to come by among Chinese people. He leaves one with the impression of a wild yak galloping from the Tibetan Plateau with indelible force and speed. I've categorized him within the vast ocean of Chinese people because he often commutes between their cities: Beijing, Chengdu, and Guangzhou. Had he chosen to remain at home in Kham, he might have gone unnoticed. . . . No, he would still stand out easily. Karma braids his shiny black hair into a long plait, adorns an upward-tilting moustache à la King Gesar in the shape of the Chinese character 八 [eight], has thick eyebrows above long slit eyes and, most notable of all, porcelain skin smooth and bright. Yes, I must make a note of his towering height: one meter eighty—who knows, even more.

Look, that's him: striding through piles of reinforced concrete in the city where countless buildings are embedded with glass panes reflecting piercing rays of light. Calm and relaxed, Karma the wild yak stands at a roadside thronging with crowds. Clad in simple clothes, he holds the newest digital camera in his left hand, the latest cell phone in his right, hailing a speeding taxi that brakes abruptly for him. He wiggles into the vehicle somewhat painstakingly, like the Chinese he speaks, such that the chauffeur has no idea where he came from. When he is dressed in Tibetan costume, most will recognize him as one of the fifty-six flowers representing the fifty-six ethnicities—ha, see: I might as well just describe Karma as a flower nomad, and in turn he probably wouldn't be able to grab a cab easily. Nowadays, people look suspiciously at Tibetans, especially those who are more outlandishly dressed.

My lengthy conversations with Karma took place on three occasions in the summer of 2004. Even though we'd known each other a long time, until then we had barely found the time to get together for a good chat. Our first "formal" conversation took place during a sun-basked afternoon, the other late at night amid barking dogs. The compound east of Lhasa was a very interesting place. Karma's elder brother rented rooms on the third story to families from Kham and greater Tibet, each with stories that appealed to me. A family from rural Kham in particular, who came to Lhasa through another brother of Karma's, caught my attention with their fascinating account of salvaging Terma scriptures with computers and modern printers. But not everyone had stories as enthralling as Karma's: Even his business card, printed with charming, delicate Tibetan antelopes on one side and the four characters DZI BEADS FROM TIBET on the reverse, seemed to offer merely a glimpse of his distinct identity.

Pressing the red button "Record" was effortless. All I had to do was to ask a question and Karma would relate stories one after another in his Tibetan-syntax Chinese. They were all so captivating, like the string of precious, expensive *dzi* beads under his collar. Whenever he felt that his awkward Chinese fell short of conveying the mystery and charm of each story—he had only started to learn the language at age twenty—he would switch channel to the sonorous and forceful Kham Tibetan language. Fit as a fiddle, he too instantaneously transformed into someone else.

Yet my tape recordings run and stop erratically, never once complete at a stretch, so whenever I rewind them, I can't help but feel it a pity. To me, Karma resembles more of a fictional character from a long novel like the Spanish-language classic *One Hundred Years of Solitude*. What a waste to portray him as just a personage in one of my other creative nonfiction pieces! Over and over I listen to his recordings. Each time they stop, I burst into laughter, just as I did when in Karma's company. I've laughed way too much, oscillating from surprise, amazement, disbelief... to profound respect and admiration. Yes, to write about someone is to follow his voice and trace the events or scenes—at once fateful, stabbing, and heartening—deeply engraved onto his life. Each place or name is no different from every teardrop and peal of laughter. This may be why from the outset Karma has imparted to me his words of wisdom: "I've never been to Hell, so I don't know how scary Hell is. But I've gone through much suffering. I've never been to Paradise, so can't tell how splendid Paradise is. But I've often known happiness."

Yet what holds me back is the challenge of editing a transcript of thirty thousand words into some mundane essay. How on earth am I going to convey the unique Karma, who appears as different personages in these interviews? How does a *tsongba* who sells *dzi* transform into an environmentalist, who from time to time blurts out trendy sound bites such as "sustainability" and "globalization"?[2]

To tell the truth, I've been worrying whether the Karma I depict in writing is indeed the Karma I know in flesh and blood. Much as the stories I jot down are indubitably his, might the Karma whom I paraphrase betray the real-life man? I might as well just change his name to something else, say Dorje or Tashi. But do I need to do that? After all, a name like Karma is rather common and banal among Tibetans; pronounced and translated into Chinese, it means either "star" or "career." I've forgotten which applies to him.

DZI, NINE-EYED STONES OR HEAVENLY PEARLS

Dzi is a Tibetan word. Is there any Tibetan who doesn't know what it is? And let me introduce its two other well-known names: One has become a fashion item today, *dzi* beads; the other is the rustic but wondrous nine-eyed stone. In fact, I really like the name "nine-eyed stone." Nine eyes and stones connected—how mythical it sounds. Doesn't it? From what I recall, there was a nine-headed demon in a King Gesar story from my childhood. I had also seen on a *thangka* a female protector and goddess, Ekajata, with only one eye, one tooth, and one breast.[3] The so-called *dzi* beads look flashy, and although Karma is known as the "King of *Dzi*," I find it too blunt a label. But for Tibetans, however nine-eyed stones and *dzi* beads are called, it is the word *dzi* that emits an unusual kind of power. As Karma explains rather simply, "Some people prefer clothes worth several tens of thousands of yuan, while others are comfortable with very ordinary clothes. . . . But no one can be compared to the one adorned by a good *dzi*. Even a Toyota Desert King is nothing next to the nine-eyed *dzi*. There exist only 200,000 *dzi* beads in the world." *Dzi* are so magical: You just have to say the Tibetan word *dzi* and everyone seems to fully understand it. Your heart yearns for it, oh . . . I've heard so, so many *dzi* stories.

Some claim that *dzi* is a kind of transformed insect that drills out of the ground before it vanishes at lightning speed—you have to grab it quickly and cover it with a hat. Some say *dzi* are treasures from deities in Heaven; after the deities were banished, the *dzi* fell to earth from those lofty places. To this day, Tibetans widely believe that *dzi* are precious stones descended from the sky. Come to think of it, aren't *dzi* in some way meteorites? The most fantastical explanation of *dzi* I've heard is that it was a treasure left by deities from Heaven and beyond—those pale, sickly deities with huge heads sitting in a boat with dharma wheels, descending from the clouds or ascending from the top of a mountain. (Let me add, the Tibetan word for "airplane" means "boat in the sky" when translated into Chinese. Could this bear any relation, however remote, to *dzi* and its deities?) Prior to their departure from the profane realm—I'm not sure if this was intentional or unconscious—the deities left behind an abundance of these mysteriously powerful *dzi* beads.

How powerful are these beads?

Legend has it that there once lived a demon called Rahula in the heavens. It boasted of nine heads with a body entirely covered in eyes. Its body a snake, it carried a bow and arrow in its hands. Every day it would shoot an arrow down to the world. Whoever hit would be paralyzed on the spot. Only a *dzi* could block this arrow before the bead broke into two. Many Tibetans enjoy wearing broken *dzi* beads with mended pieces that are glued together again: Does this mean they were once shot to paralysis by Rahula?

No doubt Karma has handled thousands of *dzi* over the years and is considered an authority in this field. He has a commanding voice, his words well founded. When it comes to mysteries and the mysterious, however, one needs to adopt another view of the world. Well, even my simple mind can grasp that. Resembling a laborer from an archaeological site, Karma puts on a grim facial expression and says to me in his fluent Kham Tibetan, "*Dzi* are mentioned in many texts and stories of King Gesar. Namkhai Norbu, a Tibetologist living outside Tibet, wrote about *dzi* in a volume about Bon religion and the ancient Shang Shung.[4] According to his research, as long as Bon religious teachings survive, so do *dzi* beads. Further, in line with Bon history and calculation, their religion has existed for more than fifteen thousand years. So you can see, the history of *dzi* can't be a mere three or four thousand years old as has been widely claimed. *Dzi* is man-made, not of this age but from a previous era. Just as the Buddhist stupa in Nepal wasn't constructed during the time of Shakyamuni, Buddhist teachings claim that it has existed since the era of the Dipamkara Buddha.[5] But I dare not say that *dzi* is confined only to Tibet: A few years ago, *dzi* was discovered in a Buddhist cave in Afghanistan. True to Shang Shung and Persian cultures, *dzi* is possibly associated with Persian tradition too. In any case, even if one could ascertain with modern science and technology that *dzi* beads were not produced in recent times, they contain elements that are now extinct. Sadly, the mode of *dzi* production is also a lost art."

Regardless of any rational—or even illogical—explanation, what exactly does *dzi* have to do with Karma? Let me begin by telling you something about Karma's hometown: a typical Khampa enclave named Gonjo in the faraway region of Kham in eastern Tibet.[6] Literally, "Gonjo" stands for a "wish-fulfilling place of treasures" where one can practice "ten virtuous precepts." Khampas from Gonjo are known as the most devout Buddhists of Tibetans, the fiercest of robbers, and the noblest of warriors. Above all, most of them are versatile businessmen. Countless stories about karma, as told by the Khampa Karma, take place in Gonjo villages.

One of them depicts a huge cypress tree at the source of the brook running by the door of a house. Karma revealed to me: "This is our family's sacred tree. It's possibly thousands of years old. Since the early times, our forefathers would hold an annual ceremony to protect this old tree. We call it *Lha-shing*, spirit tree. If its leaves hadn't changed their colors with the seasons, if they'd yellowed or withered out of the blue, it meant that a disaster might befall the family. When that happened, we invited a lama over to recite special prayers."

Every evening, Karma's father boiled a generous pot of meat, cheese, and barley to share with beggars from near and far who gathered at their home.

Child beggars from those days are now rich grown-ups, but they've never forgotten Karma's father's delicious food. Old villagers chanted *Nying-je* nonstop,[7] even though prayers and Buddhism were forbidden during the revolutionary era of the People's Commune.

Soon forty, Karma had known *dzi* ever since a tender age. For a Tibetan, and especially a Khampa, not to know *dzi* is laughable. As a matter of fact, he'd seen the treasured *dzi* secretly kept in his childhood home, but hadn't dared to see more of them or show them off outside: If a cadre had discovered the *dzi*, misfortune would befall. Karma grew up with *dzi* in his dreams. When the time was right, *dzi* would appear before his eyes for him to admire and share with others. Here came Karma's first opportunity: In 1991, he was in Xining on sheepskin business when he encountered an Amdo Tibetan by chance. The latter asked, "I've heard of something called *dzi* bead. Do you know anything about it?" Karma nodded and replied, "Yes, let's go and take a look." As it turned out, they met a *dzi* seller who was a Han Chinese man from Xining. His *dzi* bead possessed three eyes and a double circle.

"How exquisite—its three eyes," Karma exclaimed in admiration. He took a liking to it as soon as he set eyes on it and was enticed to propose a high price. Little did he realize that the two men were ganging up against him. Bought for eight hundred yuan, the *dzi* was originally from the countryside. Naively, Karma proposed twenty-five thousand yuan. In hindsight he recounted, "At that time, nobody knew how to trade *dzi*. No one knew much about *dzi*. Word soon spread about the high price I paid for the *dzi*—it caused quite a sensation throughout Xining. And as a result, many people brought me their *dzi*, authentic or fake."

What an irony: karma, cause and effect. Karma, who suffered such a loss on his first *dzi*, ended up attracting a steady stream of *dzi*. His business soon took off.

Karma's first "client" was Taiwanese. Actually, many of his subsequent sellers were Taiwanese. Apparently the Taiwanese are madly superstitious about *dzi*; they call them Tibetan *dzi* beads based on the marking and lines, the number of eyes—one, nine, or even thirteen—and other similar images or patterns such as treasure vase, lotus flower, tiger tooth, thread of pearls, lightning, thunderbolt pattern. And they lay claim to all kinds of inconceivable miraculous powers. Yet these Taiwanese "clients"—they travel all the way to Tibet to buy the "real thing" from Tibetans—have hardly the faintest idea of *dzi*'s authenticity. A Taiwanese man in the guise of a Tibetan name, Sonam Danpo, paid Karma 14,500 yuan for a wreath of two-eyed *dzi*. Then came another buyer who did not pay a cent but took Karma's *dzi* beads back to Taiwan to verify their authenticity. A month later, he returned with not just money but also the desire to purchase more *dzi*.

Naturally, there were also many Taiwanese "customers" who sought out other Tibetans to sell their *dzi*. But given their low price pressure—sometimes as little as a few hundred yuan—Karma was reluctant to sell *dzi* so cheaply. He came up with an idea to purchase as many *dzi* as possible, thereby controlling the market price, keeping it much higher than Taiwanese buyers would. Tibetans who wanted to sell *dzi* waited in long queues to do business with Karma, who ended up buying over 7 million yuan worth of *dzi*. The most lavish *dzi*, for example, cost him 600,000 yuan. But Karma did not have that much money, in fact: More than half of his money came from loans and interest rates were exorbitant. This said, Karma succeeded in controlling the market; the price of *dzi* beads soared in Taiwan. Before long, a book about *dzi* appeared in Taiwan: It featured a photo of Karma, who was now conferred the title "King of *Dzi*."

Countless *dzi* beads acquired from that time have since been sold, but Karma kept the best *dzi* for himself. Albeit with the price of the most expensive *dzi* appreciating over a million yuan, it's still a rare commodity worth keeping. Karma's rationale: A Song dynasty porcelain bowl could be bought for 10 million yuan, a Persian carpet might fetch sky-high prices . . . but the price of a *dzi*—no matter how high—can never match its real value. Not only does *dzi* possess magical and mysterious powers; it also testifies to Bon religion and history and the traditions of people from earlier times. Karma believed in researching *dzi* with the most updated scientific methods and technology. Like an anthropologist, he wrote about *dzi* tradition and culture and frequently took part in auctions. He explained, "As long as prices stay exorbitant, the *dzi* market will improve." By then, our dear Ruka Karma Samdrup was hired by the Beijing University for Nationalities as a professor specializing in precious stones. Never once had he doubted his *dzi* passion.

GO TO LHASA, TRAVEL FAR AND WIDE

To be honest, Karma's *dzi* bead stories do not intrigue me as much as his other adventures. As a writer, what stories from Karma should I use for this piece? I don't think I'm simply writing a piece about him. Just listening to his Lhasa experiences moves me to tears. Most of all, his stories teach us something about his philosophy in life: *Ley gyumdey*.[8]

Story One: Like thousands of Tibetans, Karma had dreamed of going to Lhasa since he was a child. But his parents were reluctant; after having gone through so many difficulties during the Cultural Revolution, all they wanted now was to stay home and farm and tend to their herds, take teachings from the Rinpoches and lamas in the monastery. "As long as we have enough to eat and wear, what more to ask?"

But how could Karma stifle his Lhasa dream? At eighteen, he left home on horseback and hitchhiked, first on a FAW Jiefang (Liberation) truck from the county seat to Chamdo, then squeezed with forty-two other passengers in another Liberation truck to Lhasa, tackling one flat tire at a time. Karma reminisced, "It took us ten days to get from Chamdo to Lhasa. Every night I slept on the ground. . . . I just bundled myself in a fur coat and fell asleep. It was a harsh winter, yet none of us felt the chill. Probably we were too eager to get to Lhasa, so in our excitement we'd forgotten the cold."

What does Lhasa symbolize for Karma after all?

I wonder off tangent. For these Tibetans who had never seen Lhasa, how else would they realize their wish had come true at long last, if not for the unmistakable Potala Palace burning under the majestic sun, rushing to their longing eyes like an eternal ball of fire . . . . . .

"When the truck reached the towering bridge of Lhasa," Karma continued, "I could already see Tse Potala from afar.⁹ I was ecstatic. Tears started to stream." After getting out of the truck, Karma headed straight for the Barkhor. He kept asking for directions in his Gonjo Tibetan, "How do I get to the Barkhor? Where is Tsuglakhang?"¹⁰ Whatever direction people indicated, he followed. Suddenly, he found himself walking in the crowded Barkhor, where he loitered for a while before arriving at the Jokhang Temple. As he recalled, he said, "Oh, you can't imagine how overjoyed I was. Bursting into tears, I prostrated three times and completed three circumambulations. Oh happiness! I must have cried at least two, three times that day."

As if to make sure that I'd understood him fully, Karma repeated himself, not in his limited Chinese but in Tibetan. These experiences stirred in his body, his memories of them alive. With tears in his eyes, he kept chanting *Gawo chong, gawo chong*, "happy, happy."

Story Two: After arriving in Lhasa, Karma went on a pilgrimage with his fellow villagers. Their pilgrimage lasted half a year. One of his fellow travelers was a seventy-year-old man who suddenly collapsed during their visit to Sakya Monastery. Apparently, the old man hunted a great deal in his younger days and deeply regretted his acts later in his life. At his death, he left a message: "In my past I took many lives, accumulated countless sins, and never thought of dying while on a pilgrimage, but this must be the best thing that could happen to me." Karma recalled a saying back home: If a funeral ceremony took place at the same location of death, how different would a man be from a dead dog? So Karma decided to take the old man's corpse to the sky-burial site at Sera Monastery. This meant a car ride of more than three hundred miles from Shigatse to Lhasa. Who would agree to drive or take a dead body with them on the road?

Karma wrapped the corpse in a blanket and claimed that it was beef. With luck, he managed to flag down an Isuzu truck. That was in early 1989: "Riots" had erupted, and policemen were everywhere, with armed inspection checkpoints stationed along the way. Their Isuzu truck passed through seven checkpoints, each a hair-raising ordeal in which soldiers turned the bundle over, again and again.

"How very strange," exclaimed Karma. "The bundle was flipped over so many times, but it wasn't once opened. My God, had it been opened, it'd have all been over. None of us knew any Chinese. We didn't even have a death certificate for this old man. Who could explain why the bundle contained a dead man?"

Karma carried on describing his fear and helplessness: He could do nothing but pray. He chanted Guru Rinpoche and Dolma prayers and prayed to a lama from his hometown,[11] asking them to bless him with their powers and help him get through the crisis. His prayers were answered: All seven checkpoints waved them through and they made it to Lhasa, safe and sound. Karma evoked his joy, not of someone who'd died and found Nirvana, but as though the old man had come back to life. He paid the driver an extra fifty yuan. Perplexed and amused, the driver accepted the money. On the third day, the corpse was sent for its sky burial.

Story Three: After the pilgrimage, Karma ventured into business. He traveled to the grasslands of northern Tibet, where he could sell clothes and general goods, buy wool from shepherds, as well as sheepskin and cashmere. He planned to sell them at profitable prices back in the capital, Lhasa. Once Karma traveled to the Nyima region of Ombu County to purchase cashmere from two brothers richest in their stock. At that time, government rules had stipulated that all livestock could only be sold to state-owned companies. Even if market prices were five or six times higher, it was considered illegal to sell anything to private businessowners. The two elderly brothers dared not strike a deal with Karma until they spotted the long sword around his waist, at which point they agreed to barter five *jin* of cashmere for Karma's sword.[12] Since they did not trust Karma's weighing scale, they fetched theirs instead.

Karma began to smell something fishy: How could such a huge bag of cashmere weigh no more than seven or eight *jin*?

"That can't be right," Karma argued. "This should easily weigh more than ten *jin*. Something must be wrong with your scales."

Exasperated, Sangay the farmer refused to believe Karma and told him that he bought his scale from a legitimate shop. As it happened, his scales were kilogram scales, but not one soul was aware then that a kilogram scale existed alongside a *jin* scale. Nor did Karma know anything about it. He simply went ahead and weighed the bag, this time with his *jin* scale. Indeed, there was a marked difference.

"Ah, poor old Sangay who mistook his kilogram scale as a *jin* scale," Karma sighed. "By then he'd sold so much cashmere, mutton, and sheepskin, mostly to private companies. Imagine the losses he'd incurred so far. Holding onto my neck, he cried and claimed me as his 'destined son.' In the end, he didn't just sell me all the cashmere he had at home, he also gave me five *jin* of cashmere and tons of lambskin."

Story Four, Five, Six . . .

I guess three stories suffice to prepare us for the fact that things have not gone smoothly for Karma these recent years. Quite the contrary: He has suffered greatly and was twice subjected to injustice. But I won't nag or repeat what's been said before, even though I'm sure the details could make this piece juicier! After all, this involves the dark side of bureaucracy: When all is said and done, what's there to expose the undying shadows enveloped in power? Too complicated, too sensitive, too delicate. . . . Since it's all over now, the "born-again" Karma is determined to cast this weight off his mind and move forward. Well, then, let me "give some face" to those dubious authorities who once gave Karma such a horrible time.

I must share a little about how I came to know and befriend Karma. In May 1998, I flew from sunny Lhasa to an overcast Chengdu. Chengdu is just next door to Tibet, but it was then too late for me to drop my bags at a friend's house. Right across from her place, I happened to come across a group of Tibetans at the compound gate of the Chenghua District Government. Sitting on the ground strewn with newspapers, mats, and plastic sheets, they looked tired in scruffy clothes. Still, it was clear to any stranger how angry and aggrieved they were. It was still early in the summer, but the weather was hotter and more humid than expected. Damp moisture turned into beads of sweat on their foreheads; how could these Tibetans who were used to mountainous areas bear this heat? Each behaved as if he were some noble brave horseman in his hometown. I wanted to find out what was going on, so I went over to talk to them. Right then and there, Karma appeared from nowhere, carrying two boxes of mineral water . . .

As it turned out, these Tibetans worked in the caterpillar fungus trade.[13] Most came from the Kham eastern part of Tibet; some were Amdo Tibetans from the Ngaba grasslands. The year before, they'd brought over ten thousand *jin* of caterpillar fungi collected from more than seven thousand families from various villages. Upon their arrival in Chengdu, they began to contact potential clients. A pharmaceutical company operating under the Chenghua district government swiftly responded: They confirmed receipt of their goods and promised payment at a later date. When the time came for payment, however, the owner of this pharmaceutical company was nowhere to be found. And ten thousand *jin* of caterpillar fungi disappeared with it.

With 40 million RMB up in smoke, these traders burned with impatience and fury. These traditional businessmen had obtained the caterpillar fungi from their fellow villagers who had trusted them with their livelihoods. The villagers invested so much time and toil in growing caterpillar fungus and were looking forward to their payment from the traders. While some were paid on the spot, most lived on meager means and had literally invested their homes in their caterpillar fungi. In addition, over 5 million yuan came from poverty alleviation loans in rural areas, and more than 150 million yuan were bank loans. As the last straw, the traders practically moved into the Tibetan bureau in Chengdu, hoping that someone would show up and pay their debts. Nothing happened after a few months, so they resorted to a sit-in. More than sixty businessmen were presumed to have participated in the sit-in. But how was a sit-in going to resolve the issue? Who could make up for the loss of 40 million yuan? Chenghua district authorities? Chengdu city officials? The Sichuan Province administration? Reportedly, a businessman from Ngaba named Dorgyi killed himself out of despair.

Was Karma one of the swindled businessmen?

I remember how he looked then: faintly thinner, and with a shorter pigtail tied with a rubber band. Unable to suppress his anger whenever he spoke, he frowned easily. How different he was from the present-day Karma, who now chuckles or laughs. I soon found out that he, like me, had run into the aggrieved Tibetan traders by chance. Karma believed in ethnic unity and affection. He gave up his business and became socially engaged: He delivered water, medicine, and food to them and networked widely to campaign for their cause. In the end, his hard work paid off. After some setbacks, Karma managed to be in touch with Phuntsok Wangyal, a Tibetan residing in Beijing. Although he had retired from his post as deputy director of the State Ethnic Affairs Commission, Phuntsok Wangyal still wielded authority and prestige: As the first revolutionary from Tibet, he was a famously devout

Nationalist. Why wouldn't he lend a hand? I heard that he brought the issue up with Premier Zhu Rongji. News soon circulated among provincial departments in Tibet, Sichuan, Qinghai . . . and all the way to Chengdu. It took three years for the swindled Tibetans to receive compensation. Of course, I only found out more about this much later on.

In the summer of 2002, I returned from a pilgrimage to Mount Kailash, the most sacred mountain of Tibet, where at a private banquet I ran into Karma again. I was surprised to hear him discuss environmental protection matters in Tibetan areas and the ways that policymakers should reconsider local Tibetan interests. At the banquet, Karma was introduced as one of the founders and sponsors of the pioneering Tibetan environmental organization Three Rivers Environmental Protection Group.

Fascinating, isn't it: How did he become an environmentalist? Since when has environmental protection been in vogue among Tibetans?

ENVIRONMENTALISM ISN'T A NOVELTY

I invented this catchphrase when "interrogating" Karma during his interview, only to be rebuffed by Karma himself: "I didn't just engage in environmentalism out of the blue," he explained with a smile. "Environmentalism has always been part of our own history and culture. Long ago, every monastery, clan, and important household owned its own sacred precinct, mountain, lake, river source, ancient tree. . . . It's like our natural reserve. Take for instance the cypress in our family: It symbolizes our family soul. Needless to say, we must devote all our attention to it, protect it at all costs. We've been observing this tradition for generations."

Karma's family hails from an ancient tribe from the Kham region in eastern Tibet. The tribal name, Ruka, is analogous to the nomadic culture from the past. A dispute between nomadic tribes is known as *rutse*. Farmers living on the grasslands put up tents called *rubo* for their homes and even their temples. For these nomadic people, hunting is a source of livelihood. Karma speaks for his own people: "It's a sustainable way of hunting. . . . It isn't really a massacre . . . certainly not like the ones you see in movies! We don't kill as we wish; we kill only to have enough to eat. Also we kill only male creatures . . . the ones that seem more mature, not the younger ones. We won't touch a female because it might be pregnant. This has been our nomadic custom for centuries."

Tibetan traditions stem back to Tibet's original religion, Bon, which believes in spirits and three zones of the universe—Heaven, Earth, and the

Underworld, each a place for two kinds of living beings: gods and deities, man and animals, ghosts and spirits. These living beings are capable of a myriad of metamorphoses and fantastical imaginings. Until now, Bon religion holds a strong influence on Tibetans in profound ways; Karma's family "spirit tree" must have divined his destiny and his family's eventual fate. Buddhism arrived in Tibet over 1,400 years ago. Compared to Bon witchcraft, it was viewed as more "modern" in thought, its emphasis on taking care of all living things and living a life based on "cause and effect." In Karma's words, "The six cycles of *ley gyumdey* are more effective than any harsh law. Your law may execute criminals, you can intimidate others however you wish, but *ley gyumdey* will follow you into your next life. Isn't there a Chinese saying, *You reap what you sow*? *Ley gyumdey* is both the seed and its fruit: Whether you do good or bad, it'll always follow you. So the best one can do in life is to show compassion, the worst is to take lives—shouldn't we apply this concept to our present-day politics and policies on environmental protection?"

As a child, Karma could neither afford nor find books to read. Precious texts in his family written with gold powder and silver were destroyed during the years of revolution. Karma craved literacy. He resorted to picking up the remaining torn pieces of *Tibet Daily* used by township officials to roll their cigarettes. And he read these torn fragments as though they were priceless treasures. Because of the strong influence of his Tibetan heritage, Karma's poor education did not constrain him. On the contrary, he was physically and mentally stronger than we who'd undergone the dark, narrow channel of modern education. He once shared with me that "Tibet has a deity known as Yida, the protector of all animals and plants in the mountains. When people hunt for leopards, foxes, wolves, and other wild animals, they offend Yida. Illness or difficulties might befall them. This too explains why ordinary folks do what they can to protect mountains and rivers in their home areas. At the end of the day, those living in the larger Tibetan areas have never made any distinction between the environment and animals: All living beings are equal. While the concept of environmental protection is being promulgated by developed countries, it is already deep-seated in various Asian cultures, our own Tibetan tradition included."

The Three Rivers Ecological and Environmental Preservation Group was founded in 2001, in Yushu Tibetan Autonomous Prefecture in Qinghai Province. Karma was named its secretary-general. But frankly, this title wasn't quite right, either. Since the founding of the environmental organization, Karma had spent more than a year and all his own money on it. Things began to improve over time, with funds and other sources of income to alle-

viate the expenses. Even though the funds raised were no more than a drop in the ocean, they were better than nothing. Environmental protection was barely a new concept, but an environmental organization was. In order to familiarize himself with the operations of Chinese and international organizations, Karma attended regular trainings and conferences, the most interesting of which took place at the United Nations. I'll come to that soon.

In short, with more "diplomatic" dealings underway, Karma's horizons were broadened. He discovered, for instance, "the best way" to "operate" environmental organizations: project-specific fundraising. In China, such long-term projects are more likely to drain time, money, or resources than sustain their investment. But Tibetan locals work differently from their Chinese "neighbors": They spend little to get things running. For Tibetans, environmental protection is no more or less than a cultural heritage: It needs neither science nor technology. It does not need capitalism. Some also believe that the Tibetan instinct for environmental preservation stems from its Bon tradition. And this is how Karma's environmental organization differs from others.

Karma's environmental organization has since been working on several projects, one of which campaigns against using the fur of endangered animals. The project was approved in 2002. Hunting for fur, a popular but cruel practice, is prevalent in almost all areas of Tibet. Karma criticizes, "Nowadays, Tibetans enjoy wearing tiger, leopard, otter, and fox fur. But mind you, it's a recent trend and was once forbidden in Bon tradition. Even in the past, very few elites were entitled to such privileges, so to speak. So how did it degenerate into such a crazy fashion? During the horse-racing festival of the 'Grand Celebration,' foreigners and tourists from inland China took tons of pictures of Tibetans wearing fur, then published and posted them everywhere, bragging about it as our 'national dress.' The naive locals thought they would look smart wearing animal skins, so went to buy them. You see, the tourists created a demand for fur among us Tibetans, who could never quite resist ongoing pressure from the outside world. This is a classic example of how they paradoxically and actively worked to create a 'virtual' demand. An international environmental NGO member once asked me, *Isn't it typical for Khampas to wear tiger and leopard skins?* I replied, *Absolutely not. There is no historical precedent for this . . . . It's only happened in the last ten years or so.* The NGO then suggested we apply for a grant to stop this harmful practice. And I applied. So far we've been doing quite well . . . ."

Karma stopped. He noticed a photo of *mani* stones on the table and started to chant *Om mani padme hum*. Snakes and frogs were carved onto these *mani* stones, he said. Someone who had killed snakes or frogs must have dedicated the *mani* stone to these creatures, in hope of redemption.

If I recall vaguely, Karma added, "I've forgotten almost all about business now, but I can't do without money. When I run out of money, I'll sell a *dzi* bead."

Dzi beads are known as a "virtue," a Chinese character meaning "treasure." Sources claim that a Terton once retrieved *dzi* beads with all sorts of eyes.[14] Does this imply that Karma the "King of *Dzi*" is a Terton with extraordinary skills? Or is he none other than a *dzi* himself, once hidden in the vast land of Tibet, only to be discovered by his own folks centuries after?

When a precious *dzi* is worn, as in the case of a lotus-aquarius *dzi* around Karma's neck, it protects not just the *dzi* owner but also their beloved ones from all evils and forever.

STRIKE A BELL AT THE UNITED NATIONS

In late April 2004, the United Nations planned to organize a prayer activity for world peace. Although details were vague, it had to do with a large bell gifted by the Japanese after their surrender at the end of World War II. Every year since, the United Nations has invited individuals from NGOs worldwide to "strike the bell." Until 2004, China was never invited. And by the time their invitation came, the Chinese delegates were expected to pay their own way, out of their own pockets, so few people were willing to go. Strangely, Karma was chosen. Elated and in all excitement, he rushed to Beijing to apply for a visa. In haste, he took with him the letter of invitation and nothing else. No supporting documents, no property deed or marriage certificate. Without proper paperwork, the American embassy would not grant a visa, not to mention that Karma was the least expected candidate for such a mission. But Karma did not lose heart; he carefully packed his belongings and put on light gray Tibetan clothes from the best tailor in Lhasa. His clothes were simple but stylish, their workmanship exquisite: a golden silk diagonal lapel shirt adorned by a discreet azure silk belt, and to top it off, an eye-catching long braid that gave Karma his noble and exotic look. Who could know what came to a visa officer's mind? And could he exercise objectivity in all cases? To cut a long story short, how peculiar: While the few who were most unlikely to have been refused a visa were turned down, Karma, just after applying once and without saying more, was granted one.

As a symbolic act, striking a bell isn't for everyone. Each delegation was allowed two representatives. Two young girls were initially sent to represent China, one of them an official's daughter who had been studying in America for years. This was obviously an official arrangement. Yet in the end, Karma was tacked on as an interim member. When did he begin to attract attention? Was it his Tibetan dress that brought him good luck? I've mentioned Karma's striking looks: Even without those handsome Tibetan costumes, his astonishing height and aura must have made him stand out from the others. I apologize if I've given anyone the wrong impression that I'm making an ethnic discrimination based on appearance. This isn't what I mean: I'm simply trying to make a comparison, that's all. As for those UN officials, who have they not encountered in their work? What could be so remarkable about Karma's Tibetan costume?

Meanwhile, groups of exiled Tibetans were gathering outside the United Nations every day. Among them were three young Tibetans who protested against Chinese colonial policies in Tibet. They had been on a hunger strike for more than forty days. This could be the reason Karma was selected to strike the bell: to show the world that "everyone in Tibet was very happy." Karma was given only enough time just to strike the bell once, but he was swift enough to fasten a *khata* to the top of the yellow bell, a gesture that lent the annual ceremony an "ethnic" flair. Like a charismatic star, he slowly rolled up his long sleeves, placed his hands together, and recited a short prayer, which won a warm round of applause.

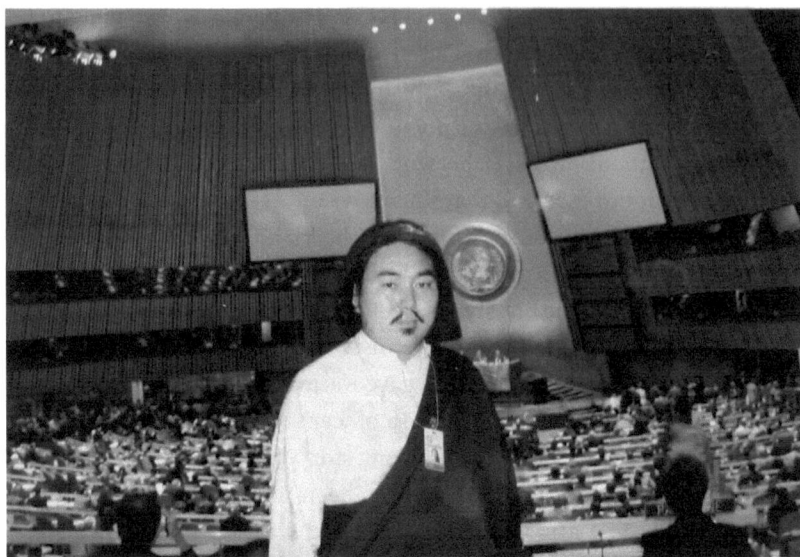

The UN officials then went around shaking the delegates' hands. When it was Karma's turn, he did not behave like the others. Instead of extending his hand politely, he acted like a juggler, took out one *khata* after another from his costume, and threw them into the air. Each *khata* unrolled and drifted like a white cloud to be steadily caught by his other hand. Next, he conveyed his best wishes in Tibetan and, with a smile, placed the *khata* around the neck of each official.

"I've lots of *khatas* in my belly," he joked.

As it turned out, other than *khatas*, Karma had books "in his belly." One of them was his loyal contact Phuntsok Wangyal's book of philosophy, *Liquid Water Exists on the Moon*. Even though Karma understood nothing of it, he held Phuntsok Wangyal in high regard. He also took the opportunity to present an illustrated brochure about his environmental NGO.

The UN officials were fascinated by this Tibetan who spoke and acted with such originality before their eyes. Journalists stopped and watched. What splendid footage. In no time, Karma was inundated by the bright glare of flashbulbs. He brought along a *thangka* intended for the then Secretary-General Annan, but Annan was not present. With deep regret, Karma entrusted the *thangka* to Secretary-General Annan's assistant.

Karma's excitement was cut short by a Chinese official. When the UN deputy secretary-general arrived, Karma again brought out a *khata* and was about to engage in "*khata* diplomacy" when the Chinese official held out his hand in a blocking motion and shouted, "That's enough! You're not allowed to do that again. What're you trying to do?"

"What do you mean?" Karma froze with the *khata* in his hand.

"Don't offer him your *khata*!"

Karma was angry. He looked straight into the Chinese official's eyes. Sternly, and in his clumsy Chinese, he said, "Offering *khatas* is our Tibetan way of showing courtesy. Even the Party leadership of the Tibet Autonomous Region offers *khatas* to superiors and foreign visitors. Now you're not letting me show Tibetan courtesy, fine, that's not a problem—I'll listen to you, but how're you going to explain this to them? Think about it."

By then the UN deputy secretary-general was bowing low, ready to receive the *khata*. Puzzled, he had no idea what was happening in front of him. The Chinese official was embarrassed; he hadn't imagined that Karma would be this stubborn. How else to resolve the stalemate but to give in to Karma?

"Fine, just give it to him."

To this day Karma insists, "Well, had I honored my Khampa sensibility, I'd have turned away and left. But I didn't—I bit my tongue and stayed on."

"How and when and where had I ever offended him? Did he envy me because I had been more popular than his daughter?" The kindhearted Karma was only willing to say this much. Truth be told, Karma did nothing wrong. He challenged the authorities, that's all: He hoped to display Tibetan courtesy, only to end up stealing the thunder of his "masters" by his side. Obviously, those "masters" were greatly displeased, which resulted in an inevitable "ethnic issue." Still, Karma's "*khata* diplomacy" proved to be a success. People remember him for his obscure environmental NGO, and that's the reason why he made the trip at his own expense. What a long way to go, just to strike a bell at the United Nations.

February 2006, Lhasa
Revised—August 2016, Beijing

NOTES

1. A Tibetan *dzi* bead is known as a "heavenly pearl" in Chinese. Karma—Karma Samdrup in full—is a businessman, philanthropist, collector, and environmentalist from Kham, Tibet (today's Tibet Autonomous Region, Chamdo Prefecture, Gonjo County). Successful in the trade of *dzi*, he is known as the "King of *Dzi*." He is also the founder of the Three Rivers Environmental Protection Group. Prior to being persecuted under false charges, Karma established a personal Tibetan cultural museum, the world's largest private collection of Tibetan artifacts. He was arrested

on January 3, 2010, and sentenced to fifteen years in prison in Shaya County, Xinjiang. Five members of his family were also imprisoned at the same time. It was a shocking injustice. Their charges were all, without exception, trumped up. The "real story" is that their good deeds offended the interest groups formed by the loathsome higher- and lower-rank officials. The suffering that Karma and his family sustained epitomizes one of the current realities in Tibet. [author's note]

2. A *tsongba* is a businessman in Tibetan. [author's note]

3. A *thangka* is a Tibetan religious painting.

4. Bon is the religion in Tibet that predates Buddhism. Shang Shung was a kingdom in western and northwestern Tibet with its own culture predating Tibetan Buddhism. The culture of Shang Shung was associated with Bon religion.

5. Dipamkara is the first of the eighteen Buddhas who existed prior to the historic Buddha Shakyamuni.

6. A Khampa is a Tibetan from Kham. [author's note]

7. *Nying-je* means compassion or empathy. [author's note]

8. *Ley gyumdey* in Tibetan refers to karma, or cause and effect. [author's note]

9. Tse Potala is the Potala Palace in Tibetan. [author's note]

10. Tsuglakhang is Jokhang Temple in Tibetan. [author's note]

11. Guru Rinpoche means "Lotus Born" in Tibetan. Dolma means the Goddess Tara in Tibetan. [author's note]

12. A *jin* is a traditional Chinese measurement unit, equivalent to half a kilogram.

13. *Ophiocordyceps sinensis*, or caterpillar fungus, is a fungus that grows on insects. In Tibetan it is known as *yartsa gunbu*, meaning "summer grass, winter worm." Gathering caterpillar fungus has become a lucrative side income for Tibetan nomads and farmers in recent years, as it is prized in China for its medicinal qualities and fetches high prices.

14. Terton means "treasure revealer" in Tibetan. In Tibetan Buddhism, a Terton is a discoverer of hidden ancient texts.

10

"Do Not Forget the Past . . ."

Do not forget the past . . .
In which night, which dream
did the moon outshine itself?
His whisper unsettles you
He has changed, he faints easily
Even the printed words have disappeared
Anguished, he leaps into a dance
with elegant gestures
no one can learn

O, under the moon, he becomes a ghost
shuffling through the temple
like a glowing key
already rusty
How can I open my Tibet?
I still scream out his daylight name
but in the day
when our paths cross
golden fallen leaves, like good days long gone
shatter under the feet!

His irretrievable face
bony features
The past, O the past is in my chest
I look back secretly
and can't help but feel startled
Suddenly, a slanted light strikes harder
like striking a large monk's robe
Dust dances
Colors flare
Tibet is beyond time

   1997, Lhasa

11

Celebrity Street Toilets in Lhasa

This story dates back at least three, four, if not five years. Which is to say I've been obsessing about toilets for that long. This is how my somewhat reliable memory has not only helped me pen down the story without omitting a word, but also sent me off to Lhasa Gonggar Airport for an adventure. Like the few plainclothes police officers trailing me around the Tibetan capital, I refused to let go of any lead. At last reaping the fruits of my field research, I finally found these toilets. With much excitement, I took as many pictures as I could of these toilets—men's and women's—and conversed in sheer delight with two farmers from Ü-Tsang on their work shifts as toilet guards.

But I'm straying off course: Wasn't I searching for Helmut Kohl's toilet? How did the other two celebrity toilets come into existence? Do toilets also have doppelgängers such that one single toilet would transform itself into two or three?

Gathering my wits, I fished out a ten-yuan bill from my counterfeit designer purse. Oh yes, you need to pay to use the toilet.

Not to fall into my bad habit of rambling here and there, let's revisit the first story I've heard. Intuiting from the two farmers' body language, I kept my ten yuan and flashed them four yuan, two yuan for each—as a small reward. Two innocent, simple-minded farmers who appeared to have emerged from a scene in Shangri-la quickly waved their hands, insisting that a yuan sufficed. Dropping the money, they then fled and forgot all about the photo we took together in front of the celebrity toilet.

The celebrity toilet for King Birendra of Nepal, off an old road to Lhasa Gonggar Airport.

KOHL'S TOILET

In July 1987, German Chancellor Helmut Kohl suggested a trip to Tibet during his visit to China. This was no small feat of diplomacy: To this day, he remains the only Western leader who has visited Lhasa. Prior to his proposal, he was chatting with Deng Xiaoping about height. Facing Kohl, who stood at 1.93 meters, the small Deng Xiaoping stated, "Even with the sky collapsing, I fear nothing. A tall man will hold it up." His words were thought to have given one the impression they had become as close as brothers.

Looking down, Kohl meant what he said. The Chinese first hid their strength to bide time before agreeing, at last, to his request. They attached great importance to this unusual trip and sped up preparations on various fronts. Exercising much care and caution, they even took into consideration the long car journey of two to three hours from the airport to Lhasa city center: What should they do if Chancellor Kohl needed to pee halfway? Surely one couldn't imagine letting the dignified chancellor of Germany perform this secret activity in public, right under the sun along the highway? So they decided to work overtime and around the clock to build a proper, functional toilet.

In view of Chancellor Kohl's massive build—he weighed over 240 pounds—the Chinese officials selected a specially solid and large-size flush toilet to import to Tibet. One couldn't help but wonder if it was imported from Kohl's hometown, or if the workers constructing the toilet were in fact members of the armed police force or the public security bureau. They were unequivocally efficient, à la Communist, such that this endearing toilet managed to be officially inaugurated at the eleventh hour. When Chancellor Kohl alighted the plane in solemnity, he was directed to Lhasa's city center, while the local Chinese host eagerly awaited his use of the much-lauded "special" toilet.

Along the way, however, Chancellor Kohl couldn't take his eyes off the scenery outside and had no desire to pee. The rivers and canyons of Lhasa were breathtaking in summer: Under the blue sky and its clouds, the Yarlung Tsangbo Grand Canyon flowed east in silence as if it had been unshaken for a thousand years. The Chinese officials calculated the distance mentally and asked cautiously, "Chancellor Kohl, do you need to pee?"

"No," replied Chancellor Kohl without turning his head around. Still a few more kilometers to go. The Chinese officials asked again gently, "Chancellor Kohl, do you need to pee?"

"No," retorted the chancellor, this time slightly displeased.

With the striking new toilet now within sight, the Chinese officials couldn't stop themselves from asking again, "Chancellor Kohl, do you need to pee?"

Visibly disturbed, Chancellor Kohl lost his temper. Allegedly wide-eyed and furious, he hurled, "*Nein!*"

From then on, everyone kept their mouths shut. To avoid a diplomatic crisis, no one ever dared to suggest toilet anymore. Days later, upon his departure, their car raced past the new toilet without Chancellor Kohl throwing a glimpse at it. Sigh, why couldn't Chancellor Kohl "give us face"? History remembers the special but unused toilet that symbolizes the Sino-German friendship, even when Kohl had done nothing more than eternalize a toilet with his name.

Thankfully the toilet wasn't demolished. I've heard how all sorts of officials, high or low, fancied an experience of the toilet tailored expressly for German Chancellor Kohl. Did they come in groups taking turns to sit on the large-size toilet bowl? In any case, officials tend to be potbellied; who knows, the large-size toilet bowl may suit their fat buttocks just right. Later, when traffic between the airport and Lhasa's city center was rerouted, a new tunnel running through the mountains, the symbol of modernity, was opened.

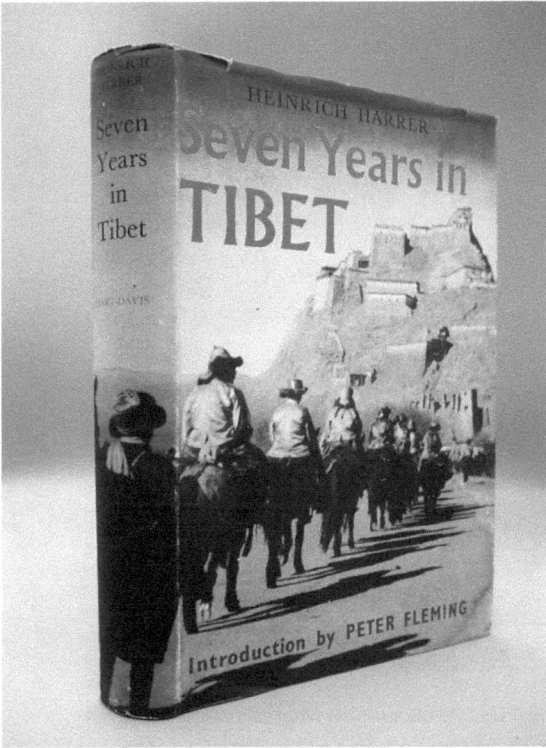

Traveling from the airport to the city is now more convenient and takes less time. Naturally, "Kohl's toilet" no longer serves any purpose. Even the large-size toilet bowl has disappeared. (Was it stolen by some curious Tibetan who would subsequently use it as a seat?) It could only be "refurbished" into an old-fashioned latrine, contracted by farmers from the nearby "New Socialist Village," and open to tourists on tours in the vicinity for one yuan per visit.

A German journalist now based in Beijing, who accompanied Kohl's team on his visit to China, narrated this story to me. He added that he'd later asked Madame Kohl why Chancellor Kohl insisted on visiting Lhasa. As it turned out, this visit to Lhasa was at that time a delicate subject: It could have easily screwed up Sino-German diplomacy, so everyone on staff was very nervous. Madame Kohl hesitated before revealing a secret: Tibet had always been Kohl's dream. When he was a child, he read Heinrich Harrer's *Seven Years in Tibet*, and since then always longed to visit the place—he felt that no matter how, he must visit Lhasa even if just once in his lifetime, even if that might risk trouble for the Sino-German relations.

Photo, Heinrich Harrer Collection (Ethnographic Museum at the University of Zurich, Inv. no. VMZ 400.07.67.036)

Harrer is none other than the famous Heinrich Harrer (1912–2006), an Austrian mountaineer who fled to Lhasa sixty years ago. He stayed on for seven years and even taught English to the young Dalai Lama. To this day, some elders in Lhasa can still recall how Harrer adored dancing and playing mahjong, that he could speak in fluent Lhasa dialect, and how particularly regal and handsome he looked when he wore Tibetan costume.

In short, Harrer was happy and very popular among the locals. But there were people who disliked him too, such as a professor and Tibetologist named Shen. He wrote about Harrer's sordid past and despicable personality and asserted that Harrer was despised by morally upright gentlemen. Of course our Professor Shen, with his bushy eyebrows and large eyes, is a perfect gentleman. Come to think of it, could he have despised our Chancellor Kohl too? Excuse me, I seem to have digressed.

This is how the mystery of life works: One must speak one's mind before a busybody—no, a selfless good soul—comes along to help. More details have since surfaced to more vividly render the image of the gigantic Chancellor Kohl.

A German-speaking friend of mine recently found on a German website a photograph of Chancellor Kohl at the time of his arrival at Lhasa Gonggar airport. Clouds and colorful flag banners fluttered in the air. The chairman of the Tibet Autonomous Region—who could know whether he was Tibetan or Chinese?—came forth to greet Kohl, and in adherence to the Tibetan protocol for greeting VIPs, he placed a white *khata*, a traditional ceremonial scarf, around Chancellor Kohl's neck. Due to the latter's height and size, we can imagine how difficult it must have been for the Communist official, who had to stand on his toes to reach Chancellor Kohl not once but twice: first to place the long scarf around Kohl's neck, then to wrap it around his neck a second time. Poor Chancellor Kohl was by then struggling just as hard to bow his head low enough for the chairman, revealing his scanty white hair on a shiny broad, bald head—

NO, KOHL DID NOT CATCH A COLD WHEN HE VISITED TIBET IN JULY 1987: This was how the news was reported in German. Isn't it wicked?

But apparently the journalist had no idea what a *khata* really was; instead, he described it as a "lovely raw silk scarf." Scarf? What a city bumpkin. The journalist added that when three lovely Tibetan girls adorned in their traditional outfit approached Chancellor Kohl offering *chang*, highland barley wine, with an intricate copper kettle and silver bowl, the chancellor was so busy shaking hands with others that he didn't even glance at them. Oh, poor beauties who were greeted with a cold shoulder: They lost a golden opportunity to sing their Tibetan wine song of friendship.

Looks like Chancellor Kohl's arrogance has indeed something to do with his peculiar personality, which was why he not only refused to use the large-size flush toilet tailored for him by the Chinese Party, he was also too lazy to even glimpse at it by the highway. One can only guess why he simply stormed away so brusquely.

During early winter, the river valleys of Tibet are chilly in both the mornings and evenings, but as soon as the sun rises, they get warmer. Trees lining the streets glow like gold in the sun. Even the five-star red flags atop the Tibetan-style dwellings—a common phenomenon of the new socialist countryside—appear crimson red. One after another, various "happiness" projects displaying the Central Committee's love for the Tibetans have been implemented; more recently, the railway line from Lhasa to Shigatse was successfully opened. Even though no information in Tibetan language is posted anywhere on the train, which frightens old, non-Chinese-speaking Tibetans, we trust that such minor "flaws" will ultimately be "resolved." We must believe in the Party's meticulous care for the "emancipated serfs." Take, for instance, a Chinese man who drove his car through the remote areas of Ngari Prefecture: He hit a *kyang*,[1] an animal listed as one of the national endangered species, then cut out its genitals while it was still alive to fry or eat raw as an aphrodisiac. In accordance with the law, the Chinese man was punished by the respective government departments, or so they say. Yet from several different sources we learn that this man has been posting photos on WeChat, showing off his theatrical act of knifing off the still-alive *kyang*'s penis. As it turns out, he was involved in mining in the Shigatse area and contracted by a railway company from Zhejiang. By no means was this man some "anonymous lumper," contrary to what the government had later announced.

Whether the road from Lhasa to Gonggar Airport is in the midst of renovation or expansion, I've no idea, save for the fact that traffic is now diverted through an old road that's been dormant for years. That, on the other hand, is quite exciting. Kohl's toilet, which I'd so far only heard about, is located just along this road; isn't that my rare chance to do some fieldwork?

So when I finally caught sight of that so-called public toilet on the road that faces somewhere west of Chushul County, I was overjoyed. On the spur of the moment, I felt a déjà vu; it seemed that I'd been on this road several times before and had even stopped here for a quick toilet break. The place felt as if it had nothing to do with the former German chancellor. Rather, it seemed related to King Birendra of Nepal, who, as you know, fell victim to the royal massacre in 2001. As expected, the two Tibetan farmers guarding the toilet confirmed what I had sensed. The elder one was shy and quiet. He held a ball of wool in one hand, a spindle in another. The wool became thinner and thinner as it wrapped around the spindle. (It's a traditional Tibetan way of spinning wool and usually a task undertaken by men.) The younger farmer, on the other hand, was open and cheerful; a smoke-stained yellow tooth protruded from his mouth, but his mustache was intricately shaped into the Chinese character /\ [eight], and he looked rather well groomed. He was wearing leather clothes and a Western-style hat and seemed to be living a happy life.

"So was this toilet built for Helmut Kohl or the Nepalese king?" I probed.

"For *Payul Gyalpo*, the Nepalese king," the yellow-toothed farmer responded.

The mesmerizing photo of King Birendra of Nepal and his wife that hung in the Barkhor shops run by Nepalese merchants appeared right before my eyes. The grievances of a royal family are as unfathomable as the ocean. I still don't understand why the king and his family on the other side of the Himalayas could have been shot dead at random. Perhaps some international detectives and the sensational paparazzi have long understood why, but not me. In November 1973, King Birendra visited Beijing. Exiled Tibetan guerrillas were active against the Chinese in the Mustang district during that time, and Mao threatened him with sending in Chinese armed forces if he did not stop them. The Mustang district stretches into Tibetan territory, and parts have been closely intertwined with Tibetan culture and fate. In reality, it was once a tiny Tibetan kingdom until it was annexed by Nepal, thus turning into a tragic site. Back then, it still enjoyed sufficient autonomy to accept fellow Tibetans who had started fleeing China in March 1959. Originally supported by the CIA, the Mustang district could not defend itself when American support dwindled. Sadly, after the establishment of formal Sino-American diplomatic relations in 1972, this support was withdrawn completely. King Birendra surrendered, which resulted in armed guerrillas causing much trouble for the Chinese. Many Tibetans died violent deaths. Never must we forget.

In any event, I have to take a closer look myself in order to find out whether the toilet was built for Helmut Kohl or King Birendra of Nepal. The "toilet building" boasts of an architectural style akin to a miniature castle's, but the solar heater and water tanks atop its roof created a distinctly modern flair. I enthusiastically hurried toward the women's toilet, but alas, how disappointing the interior was. I wasn't expecting any fancy flush toilets;

still, what I saw was simply a row of banal white porcelain squatting pans that hardly looked special. Toilet paper holders made from galvanized iron sheets were attached next to the squatting spots, and without paper. White tiles covered just a third of the walls, the remaining parts literally with stains and in pieces. How filthy. There wasn't any water to flush the toilets, which made me wonder if the water tanks behind the toilets and the wash basins en face were merely decorations. Only the heptagonal windows high up on one wall seemed rather peculiar aesthetically. Had they been maintained and cleaned, they might have actually looked pleasing to the eye.

Since King Birendra was male, I asked if I could also take a look at the men's toilet. The generous, yellow-toothed farmer agreed without ado. "No problem at all," he said. "Do as you please."

The men's toilet was equally appalling; the only difference was it included a few more squatting pans. I used my iPhone to take a couple of photos nonchalantly and left.

The yellow-toothed farmer had never met someone who was that interested in toilets. He laughed and told me I could find another toilet down the road: Jiang Zemin's toilet. I was bewildered, not least because his Mandarin was far from standard. When he said "Jiang's toilet" (pronounced as *jiang ce* in Chinese), it sounded like "Gyantse," the small Tibetan town famous for its climate and manifold resources and situated two hundred kilometers away.

Incredible! I came here to visit Kohl's toilet, but that'd turned out to be King Birendra's toilet and now, Jiang Zemin's toilet! Kohl's toilet, where are you?

TOILETS FOR KING BIRENDRA OF NEPAL AND JIANG ZEMIN

According to my online sources, King Birendra of Nepal had visited Lhasa at least twice: first in June 1975, toward the end of the Cultural Revolution, and next in May 1996, during the "reform and economic opening-up." This is how the official Chinese media, Xinhua News Agency, reported it at that time:

> Several officials from the "revolutionary committee of the TAR (Tibet Autonomous Region)" hoisted Chinese and Nepalese flags at Lhasa airport to warmly welcome King Birendra on his visit to Lhasa. [...] Crowds cheered as countless flags and banners lined the boulevard from the hotel to Potala Palace, resembling "a corridor of friendship." People from different ethnic groups dressed in their festive clothes gathered on both sides of the road. When the king left his hotel, youths started to play their

bamboo flutes and strike their waist drums [what kind of waist drums? Shaanbei waist drums? Does a Tibetan know how to play waist drums?] performing folk dances and singing songs of friendship.[2] People waved flamboyant ribbons and continuously shouted slogans, celebrating King Birendra's "successful visit" to Sichuan and Tibet and wishing for an "eternal Chinese-Nepalese friendship" . . .

Clearly the coverage was incomplete: The custom-built toilets demonstrating the special relationship between two nations were not mentioned at all. What a let-down to the goodwill of folks all the way from Beijing to Lhasa. More regrettably, no one today knew for sure if King Birendra of Nepal had graced the toilet, whether he left as legacy any word of warmth and generosity that would "promote" this special "friendship." After all, he was different from German chancellor in that a weak ruler of a Third World country was not in the same category as a political leader from a modern empire, so he couldn't have been arrogant; how else could Mao intimidate him with threats? Was his Lhasa visit just a pretext for him to report on Mustang's Tibetan guerrillas? Or was he merely trying to find out about his neighboring country's power and might?

Another report from Xinhua News Agency claimed that during his visit to Lhasa, King Birendra "watched a military performance by Lhasa's militia . . . Participants included Tibetans, Han Chinese, Hui Muslims, and the Bouyei." How could the Bouyei be possibly part of this? The report added, "Men and women alike staged elaborate anti-aircraft artillery performances such as surface-to-air missiles, foot soldiers shooting at targets in the air, a salvo of gunfire, individual soldiers resisting shots . . . Their skillful shooting and spectacular performance earned welcoming applause from the guests. At the end of the show, the performing militia ranks gathered in a single file and shouted *Long live the Sino-Nepalese friendship!*" Oh my God, did that frighten King Birendra of Nepal such that he wet his pants?

Not much could be written about King Birendra's second visit, as it paled in comparison to the first. This is all I wanted to know: Did the tradition of building toilets for celebrities along the way to Lhasa begin with the visit of King Birendra? Was the construction of a toilet for German Chancellor Helmut Kohl part of this meaningful tradition and its legacy?

In July 1990, the then–General Secretary of the Chinese Communist Party Jiang Zemin "visited Tibet on his way to inspect provinces and districts along the southwestern border." An overseas Chinese story reports, "Jiang Zemin, sixty-four, wearing an embroidered Tibetan hat and headband, inspected the region as if he was enjoying his first Tibetan expedition." Although "a team of staff carried with them oxygen cylinders, in case of emergency," Jiang "seemed to cope better than his subordinates," except when in Tashi Lhunpo Monastery, before the body of the Tenth Panchen Lama, known as the "Great Patriot," Jiang Zemin experienced sudden "breathing difficulties, while beads of perspiration appeared on his face . . . He wavered out of the hall before coughing out loud. He then sat down on a rock and put on an oxygen mask."

Although not one piece of coverage has mentioned that he too was lavished with special treatment—personal access to his special toilet—the Tibetan people will silently remember *jiang ce*: Jiang Zemin's toilet.

O, how these toilets immortalize celebrities—

WHY BUILD TOILETS FOR CELEBRITIES?

As I gaze at a surreal contre-jour photo of King Birendra of Nepal's toilet, I've long forgotten about Helmut Kohl's toilet. In fact, who cares whose toilet it is? A nobody's toilet is a toilet, a celebrity's toilet is also a toilet—all of them emit a stench of feces and are not worth a mention in the long river of history.

I asked a yellow-toothed farmer what he thought about villagers taking turns to guard this toilet. He kept saying, "Smuggle, smuggle." We burst into laughter when out of the blue he blurted out this Chinese verb. It's a loanword, very fashionable among inland Tibetans, and refers to forged and fake commodities from "Gyana," which in Tibetan means mainland China. Slightly embarrassed, and probably ashamed of his poor Chinese, he added in Tibetan, "Lies, lies."

The farmer continued to explain, "Without water, we have to go fetch water from the river with our tractor. That water tank, that tap, ah . . . smuggled, lies." Pointing to the water heater atop the toilet, he said, "This, smuggled, lies."

Back home in Beijing, I study the photograph carefully and notice a row of characters painted in white against a red background on the water heater: HUANG MING SOLAR ENERGY HEATER (HONG KONG). Since the Han character "Huang" connotes "emperor" in Chinese, this quite suits the rank of King Birendra of Nepal and by extension, is rather compatible with "smuggled" and "lies."

I consider further: Why must we—at the last minute—build toilets for visiting celebrities? Other than reasons related to precaution and safety, might there be another motive beyond providing relief for celebrities on the road? A scandalous bit of news coverage from some years back came to my mind: During Kim Jong-il's visit, the North Korean leader's urine and shit was transported back to his country so as not to have his health details leaked. Such verity must have come across to many as a joke and was described by foreign media as "a dictator's paranoia."

But not quite, in my opinion; there's more to it than meets the eye: According to the news, when Kim Jong-il visited China in January 2006, the Chinese attempted to extract his urine sample from toilet bowls where he'd sat, in order to find out more about his health condition.

Here's another true story: Former Soviet Union leader Nikita Khrushchev threw himself into writing his memoirs after retiring from the political scene, and in so doing, he exposed all kinds of secrets and behind-the-scenes information. In no time, he fell under the KGB's close scrutiny; even his toilet at home was wiretapped. In a rage, Khrushchev protested, "Have you spent so much taxes of the proletariat, just to listen to me fart?"

As the saying goes: When the fox preaches, take care of your geese—someone is always up to some evil. Whether it's a toilet for German Chancellor Kohl or King Birendra of Nepal, or even a toilet for General Secretary (and later Chairman) Jiang Zemin, it must hide something that's known to no one. After all, the urine and shit of these celebrities (who knows, their farts too) is indeed different from the urine and shit of a nobody: It's closely linked to the fall and rise of a civilization. It's a top state secret, to be classified, encrypted, and put under wraps.

But a democratic leader such as Chancellor Helmut Kohl shouldn't be considered a dictator, so why didn't he do us the honor of leaving behind his precious shit and urine, or at least grace the toilet just once? Did he also have to take into account national security?

What a convoluted issue. My ordinary brain lacks global perspective and is starting to ache. I'd better stop here.

Still, I can't help but laugh out loud when I think of villagers such as the yellow-toothed farmer and his wool-making compatriot who fetch water in their tractors from the surging Yarlung Tsangbo Grand Canyon: Did they also, like in a relay, sing folk songs from Ü-Tsang, music that celebrates productivity, while emptying buckets of river water into storage tanks atop the toilets?

Allow me to give free rein to my imagination: When a celebrity steps foot into this rather posh-looking toilet with a majestic air, is it true that farmers sprawling atop the toilets must lean their bodies as closely as they could, with breath held, so as to go unnoticed? When the celebrity heaves a long sigh of relief, his entire body now liberated, he would gradually stick out his omnipotent thumb to press on the button and flush the toilet. And no sooner must the farmers atop the toilet unlock the sluice gate without error or delay, fulfilling at last the veneer of marvelous modernization?

January 2015, Beijing
Revised—June 2016

NOTES

1. *Kyang* means means "wild ass" in Tibetan.
2. The insertion is an aside from Woeser.

12

Ocean, as Much as Rain

An "ocean" commonly refers to a silver coin, but why—and how—is it related to the ocean and, implicitly, the other shore? Although we Tibetans too refer to this silver coin as *dayang* in Chinese, we pronounce it slightly differently: The character *yang* is pronounced with an accent that slants upward as if floating in midair, yet bears no resemblance to any particular Tibetan word. Clearly, this is yet another example of linguistic mutation whereby the Chinese language is imported into Tibet. Of course, Tibet had its own currency, which was known as *tangka*. Long ago, Lhasa had started its own production of money. By the Manchu dynasty, however, the currency production in Nepal began to go downhill: What a nuisance it was to print the emperor's regnal year on every banknote and coin; why not just print one's own currency as one wished? Wasn't one the king of one's own territory?

I've lost track of the source for this information: Allegedly, the Chinese Communists carried countless silver coins during their invasion of Tibet. When they lacked the manpower to carry money with them, they loaded airplanes with coins and banknotes to drop them box by box from the air. Once, a few boxes landed in the wrong place. They were dropped right into the upper stretches of the Yangtze River before being engulfed by the torrent. All along the way, Tibetans who witnessed this, whether rich or poor, saw *dayang* sprinkling out just like rain.

Imagine the dramatic scene. Rolls of silver coins torn off their sealed thick cardboard were suddenly thrust into the air, then gradually fell from the sky, shimmering and chiming in the sun before finally hitting people on their heads in a mess.

"As much as rain!"

Those greedy Tibetans leaped for joy, dazzled, their overzealous arms wide open. But one of them observed with composure and indifference before remarking, "This is just honey at the edge of a blade. Lick the honey and your tongue will be cut."

I read about this from an account by American journalist John F. Avedon, *In Exile from the Land of Snows* (1984). The calm onlooker was none other than Taktser Rinpoche, our Dalai Lama's elder brother who later exiled to India before settling in America, where he taught at Indiana University. A strong advocate of the Tibetan independence movement, he died in 2008. Later, a man from Nyarong by the name of Jamyang Norbu sang an elegy:[1]

> First with sweet talk and glittering silver
> next with guns and death
> They plundered my fields and cattle
> set fire to the monasteries I worship, ravaging
> They killed us like crushing mole crickets and ants
> murdering my friends, kin, lamas, and those I love.[2]

Let me recount a few more instances of this enigmatic torrential rain of "oceans." To "elicit support among the nationalist elites and the patriotic upper class," the foreign liberators poured money like rain on Lhasa. The eyes of several aristocrats and merchants grew round with delight once they saw money and hastened to sell their houses, lands, food in storage, and fleece. As long as they were willing to collaborate, they were handsomely rewarded by the Chinese. Chen Zonglie, a photographer from Beijing sent to work at the newly established *Tibet Daily*, has this to say years later: "The assistant chief editor Kasho Dhondup was an aristocrat born to a well-off family and easily earned a monthly wage of more than a thousand 'oceans.' Each time he received his salary, he would send for his servant to cart home *pulu* bags of 'oceans.'"[3] Oddly, Chen made no mention of the aristocratic assistant chief editor's suicide during the subsequent Cultural Revolution. Looking at the statistics, Kasho Dhondup did not have many good days to enjoy from his fat wages. In 1956–57, all students from recently opened primary and secondary schools in Lhasa were allowed to receive thirty "oceans" every month regardless of their family background, as the government intended to invest in them to cultivate successors for the revolution. One can't say it wasn't generous, but with time the amount dwindled. Just before the outbreak of the Cultural Revolution, all a year-one student received was a mere fifteen Chinese yuan.

1959年7月13日，宣布释放自愿投诚的127名叛乱分子．
127 rebels who surrendered to the PLA are released on July 13, 1959.

Even captive soldiers from Kham during the earliest combats with the Chingdrol Magmi were not ill treated: They were perceived as "class brothers," rewarded with *khatas* and "oceans" before being sent home free. "Chingdrol Magmi" is the Tibetan for People's Liberation Army, along with the Tibetan term for "revolution," *sar jie,*[4] both of which belong to the new lexicon of "New Tibet." An old man once told me that after the battle in Chamdo, Tibetan captive soldiers were given five "oceans" each, whereas those with family and children were given three additional "oceans." Journalists who tagged along with the Communist army took pictures of these Tibetans expressing their heartfelt gratitude upon receiving their money. To this day, we can still come across such photographs in propaganda exhibitions that educate the masses about the Tibetan "liberation." Naturally, the bloody massacre that took place in the Norbulingka in March 1959 is not mentioned in any of these exhibitions.[5]

Years ago, rumors spread in Lhasa that the newly constructed Kesang Lingka district along West Liberation Road was haunted. Apparently, many Tibetans massacred in the Norbulingka were buried there like in a mass

graveyard. During the eventual construction of houses, workers dug out piles of white bones from the ground, as well as *dzi* beads, the priceless "nine-eyed agate" or sky beads; imported watches such as West End or Rolex that had stopped forever at some hour; and rusty "oceans." With the rust removed, each "ocean" still chimed when one blew it . . . Doesn't this story show that the Chingdrol Magmi weren't really stealing small items belonging to the Tibetan masses? Honestly, I believe the part about evacuated piles of white bones, but not about the valuables. Had there been any valuables, they would have long been confiscated.

COUNTRY BUMPKINS GO INTO TOWN

Since young, I've come across "oceans" in my father's antique collection. These were a scant few pieces left over from his Tibetan military zone salary. I know some inside stories from his past. During the mid-1950s, my father

carried heavy army bags full of "oceans" and bought a 120 Zeiss Ikon camera. When the Cultural Revolution took Lhasa by storm, he used the camera to photograph the destruction of the Jokhang Temple and the public persecution of "patriotic elites." I've now inherited his camera. Whenever I hold it in my hands, I can feel the weight of history. Its leathery brown exterior has been wrinkled by use and time. Even the machine itself contains prints of wear, a proof of my father's years of use. Once the lens opens, it zooms outward in light but crisp sounds. With my left eye shut, my right eye peeks out from the tiny aperture: Will I also see the "massacre" my father once witnessed? Couldn't I at least see for myself how many "oceans" it took to purchase an excellent German camera in those days?

Thinking back, the Chinese troops must have behaved like "country bumpkins going into town" during their invasion of Lhasa. They must have been dazzled by the kaleidoscopic diversity of products in the streets. As described in a memoir by a geologist who went to Tibet in 1956,

Although the Barkhor was no longer than six hundred meters, it was paved with cobblestones, gathering famed goods and brands from all over the world. Everywhere were shops full of exquisite and colorful collections of chic, luxury products: Rolex, Omega, and Longines watches from Switzerland; high-end Contax cameras and Browning pistols from Germany; daggers from Finland; Parker pens from America; Philips radios from Holland; carpets, pearls, jewelry, gold and silver, wool and fabrics from Italy and elsewhere. You could find almost anything you wanted. These products were very rare to come by in the inland market, so we hunted around in a mood of curiosity. Neither hurried nor slow, we went in and out of the shops one by one. After some probing, we realized that the products here were indeed genuine and reasonably priced. In fact, they were much more fairly priced than elsewhere, except that they were priced in "oceans" rather than Chinese yuan. This was a partial, approximate price list of our discoveries: expensive watches at 150 to 170 "oceans"; high-end cameras at 150 to 160 "oceans"; Parker pens at ten to twenty-five "oceans"; wool at six "oceans" per pound; woolen fabric at eight "oceans" per meter. Without a doubt, all these prices were cheaper than the ones in domestic Chinese and Hong Kong markets.[6]

Even in 1956, when one of the Chinese Communist founding fathers, Marshal Chen Yi, led a grand delegation of eight hundred representatives to visit and convey greetings to the army stationed in Lhasa, they were so overwhelmed by the lavish display along the Barkhor that they did not care for their pride. Instead, they spent without restraint such that the delegates had truly become the watch-wearers.[7] As the story goes, almost everyone ended up wearing brand-name watches all up their arms to bring them home as gifts for friends and kin. Needless to say, they must have exchanged their "oceans" for these high-end imported watches.

At this point, I can't help but digress a bit more: Could it be that there were so many brand-name products then in Tibetan society that were consumed by the "feudal lords"? Surely the commoners must have seen some decent days too. During the current exhibitions of "bittersweet memories of Tibet," tourists and visitors are likely to come across vintage photographs of wretched beggars from old Tibet. Truth is, I still see them in the streets of present-day Lhasa.

Not long after, the rain of "oceans" splattering across the army path began to hit the financial markets of Tibet too. "This was something that had never been experienced before and my people did not understand how the price of grain could double overnight," wrote the Dalai Lama in his second autobiography, *Freedom in Exile* (1990). In his earlier memoir, *My Land and My People* (1962), His Holiness spoke of the pain matter-of-factly: "For the first time that could be remembered, the people of Lhasa were reduced to the edge of famine." So the honeymoon enjoyed by Tibetans and their Chinese intruders lasted reluctantly and briefly before coming to an abrupt end.

UNCLE CHEN'S "OCEAN" PRODUCTION

Life brims with incredible encounters. Never would I imagine that my husband's foster father Uncle Chen had actually manufactured—or rather, mass-produced—"oceans."

I first met Uncle Chen when he was already over eighty. When he learned of my Tibetan identity, he said to me with a grin, "Fate has bound me to Tibet. Do you by chance know anything about 'Big-Head Yuan'? Well, back then I was the one who produced your 'Big-Head Yuan.'"

I was stunned. "Big-Head Yuan" is another common term for silver coins: The front side of a coin is engraved with a profile of the warlord Yuan Shikai clad in military uniform during the waning years of the Manchu dynasty.[8] His huge bald head, bushy beard, and plump shining ears became a classical emblem. Several films about the diabolical old society feature scenes of Chinese pinching a "Big-Head Yuan" with their fingertips, blowing at it, then quickly holding it close to their ears to hear the coin chime. Apparently that was a way to differentiate a real coin from a fake. Looks like forgery has a long history; one must master the martial arts of eagle eyesight and sharp ears in order to tell the difference.

Uncle Chen was an esteemed old revolutionary who enjoyed ministerial pay in his heyday. As an Eighth Route army soldier, he lived for years in shabby traditional cave houses in Yan'an, the base of the Chinese Communists after their Long March. I've always wanted to hear stories about his past and to know more about his intriguing mass production of "Big-Head Yuan." But I was lazy and kept procrastinating until four months before his death, Uncle Chen blessed me with a crash course.

At age ninety-one, Uncle Chen was ever zealous whenever he spoke of "Big-Head Yuan." It was late 1948. During the Civil War, the Communist Marshal Lin Biao won the Liaoshen Campaign at the price of 500,000 deaths on both sides, not to mention 300,000 civilians from Changchun who were starved to death. Uncle Chen, who left Yan'an for Changchun and Harbin in 1945 to mass-produce banknotes for the Chinese People's Liberation Army,

now made a detour for Shenyang to take over the Shenyang Mint from the Russians. He painstakingly narrated the details of how the People's Liberation Army produced its own currency. Wherever they fought, their currency was in use. He even evoked memories of the early years of the Shenyang Mint during the late Manchu dynasty and gave me history lessons about the relationship between the mint and Manchuria, the three provinces of northeastern China, and the Japanese, as well as the young Marshal Zhang Xueliang, who was abducted by Chiang Kai-shek and kept under house arrest in Taiwan until Chiang's passing in 1975. But since I'm not interested in these details, I'll skip over them.

"Historically, the Shenyang Mint was known for its mass-production of 'Big-Head Yuan.' Molds were preserved from the Manchu years, the mint machinery and facilities evacuated from the foundry scrap. Most artisans were summoned back to work; all was ready, save for the silver."

Uncle Chen continued, "At that time most of China was liberated. Everywhere was all about 'Down with *tuhao* [the nouveau riche], distribute the land'—have you heard about it? In less than a month, gold and silver were transported steadily from places across the country via trains and cars, in sacks and hampers filled to brim with gold and silver ingots and all kinds of silvery and golden utensils: candleholders, bowls, chopsticks, wine cups, even jewelry for women such as hairpins, clips, rings, bangles, earrings with jade or agate . . . How exquisite . . . All these were confiscated in one go. Obviously these old riches used to belong to wealthy landlords, which was why they had to all be viciously looted and destroyed."

"Gold to the banks, silver to the mint," explained Uncle Chen. "First, they melted silver in a furnace so huge that it couldn't even be carried by two or three men . . . until the silver burned into a fiery red and was melted into liquid, like in brickmaking, warehousing, or chemical tests. At that time, regulations stipulated that the contents of silver must be no less than three 'nines'—in other words, 99.9 percent. The relative purity must be fixed at the precise 99.9. We even polished up the mold print of Big-Head Yuan's worn-out epaulette. Making currency was our political mission to help prepare troops to go south. People in the south were used to silver coins. Ethnic minorities recognized only silver coins, not banknotes, so our coins had to maintain a good reputation in order to be useful in those regions.

"After inspection," Uncle Chen elaborated, "the coins were melted into meter-long strips and compressed into pieces equal in thickness before being melted again and compressed into round biscuits one by one. Hydrochloric and sulfuric acids were used to rinse out the natural silver color. Machines and gears were used to carve out the gear-teeth circumference of each piece before compressing on it the image of 'Big-Head Yuan': the front side featuring Yuan Shikai's bald head, the tails side with the characters THE REPUBLIC OF CHINA YEAR THREE. The coins were poured onto the hot brick bed to be steamed for another five or six hours so that each produced a chiming sound when one blew at it. During the final production stages, specialized paper was used to bundle fifty coins into a roll before they were packed, sealed, packaged, and carted away in numbered boxes. In those days, people were mostly well behaved. They wouldn't cheat or steal. Even if you did, there was no place to hide anyway.

"In short, our 'Big-Head Yuan' was produced mainly for the ethnic minorities. Since we were liberating ethnic minority areas, we needed the help of locals in negotiating policies . . ." Uncle Chen concluded aloud.

"To negotiate policies? Does that mean that 'Big-Head Yuan' was used to buy popularity?" I asked cautiously.

Uncle Chen smiled but did not respond.

"So the 'oceans' raining in Tibet weren't the genuine 'oceans,' but the ones you mass-produced?"

Uncle Chen replied, "But our 'oceans' contain more silver than the real 'Big-Head Yuan'!"

I wanted to chip in, "First the Communists raided their own people's homes and plundered their own houses, next they cheat on their neighbors. In the end, all were deceived on account of having more money than sense." But I held my tongue.

For years, Uncle Chen yearned to visit Lhasa. He listened to Tibetan songs, read Tibetan books, and took a keen interest in Tibetan affairs. My husband frequently treated him to authentic Tibetan meals in Beijing. Each time we met, he was eager to chat about Tibet. Shortly before his death, he was reading my husband's most recent book, *Sky Burial: The Fate of Tibet*, just published in Taiwan. Doesn't that make him the oldest fan of Tibet among the Chinese? Did his passion for Tibet have anything to do with the "Big-Head Yuan" that he mass-produced for Tibetans years ago?

A Chinese friend who had never heard of the "Big-Head Yuan" myth had learned of Yuan's war triumphs. He blurted out, "What's it got to do with the Communists who claimed to have liberated Tibetans? Isn't it obvious that Yuan Shikai the Northern Warlord liberated Tibetans?" In reality, the political task of buying popularity is still very much prevalent in Tibet. It's just that "Big-Head Yuan" is now replaced by the "Mao-Head" banknotes, and the victims are no longer "patriotic upper-class or nationalist elites," but vagrants and people from all walks of life. As long as they remain tame and obedient, *the "oceans" sprinkle just like rain.*

"OCEANS" MELTED INTO A REINCARNATED GODDESS OF MERCY

On August 24, 1966, teachers who helped in the nation-building of "New Tibet," including Tao Changsong and Xie Fangyi,[9] led Red Guards from the Lhasa Junior High School holding portraits of Mao and slogans such as ERADICATE THE OLD ROTTING WORLD, BE THE MASTERS OF THE NEW WORLD while they headed for the Tsuglagkhang, the Jokhang Temple, to destroy the "Four Olds." The students weren't the only ones destroying the temple: All work units in Lhasa were involved, including the committee members as leaders and the Lhasa neighborhood committee units for activists, the "revolutionary masses."

In a matter of hours, the open-air courtyard in the Jokhang was piled with ruined statues of Buddhas, ritual instruments, sacrificial vessels, and many other symbolic Buddhist objects. The golden apex was smashed, sacred texts burned, murals painted thousands of years ago brutally scraped off walls and reduced to mud.

Originally housed in the Tukje Lhakhang,[10] the thousand-armed and thousand-eyed Avalokiteshvara statue with eleven faces was also destroyed as a result of these unprecedented revolutionary acts.[11] Among the five destroyed statues, several Buddhas' fingers were broken off, and some *zhungzhug* were lost, but devout Tibetans took risks to collect them in secret.[12] One of these Tibetans was a Kazara who was once a monk.[13] Dawa Tsering, the current chairman of the Tibet Religious Foundation of the Dalai Lama in Taiwan, wrote me this touching story when I was working on my photo and commentary book about the Cultural Revolution in Tibet, *For-*

bidden Memory: "When the Red Guards were destroying all these treasures, a Tibetan-born Kazara who was a monk before he became a Red Guard, quietly took the Buddha's head and hid it in his home. Since he was Kazara, not Tibetan, there was little chance that his home would be searched. In Tibet, Kazaras enjoyed more privileges than Tibetans themselves . . . Although this man was a so-called 'foreigner,' he never wavered in his religious beliefs. Later, he managed to smuggle the Buddha's head out of the country and offered it to Gyalwa Rinpoche, the Dalai Lama, in the present-day Tsuglagkhang of Dharamsala." (Gyalwa Rinpoche is worshipped by Tibetans as the embodiment of Chenrezig the thousand-armed and thousand-eyed Avalokiteshvara. And Tibet is considered the sanctuary of Avalokiteshvara.)

Reportedly, five ruined Buddha faces were sent clandestinely to Dharamsala in two batches. As narrated by the Dalai Lama in his *Dharamsala Mahayana Buddhist Tsuglagkhang Historical Records* written account, "Tibetans one by one found a way: Out of five faces of Avalokiteshvara, someone took a wrathful and a peaceful face, and in 1967 passing to someone

else, they reached India through Nepal. In 1968, another wrathful face, along with a head of the Amitabha Buddha, made it to India through Nepal under similar circumstances."

In 1969, during the construction of the eleven-faced thousand-armed-and-eyed Avalokiteshvara in the temple that shared the same name in Dharamsala and Lhasa, the Dalai Lama summoned the sculptor and handed him the five ruined statue faces, asking him to put three of them within the re-molded statue head. As the seventh page notes, "The three heads were filled with *zhungzhug* following the same religious rites according to the texts, therefore for those devotees who go to make offerings, it is no different to the Avalokiteshvara in the Tsuglagkhang in Lhasa." Since the other two faces needed no repair, they were placed next to the remolded statue, as a warning about the catastrophic Cultural Revolution. Along with the lost *zhungzhug*, the inside was remolded, while the remaining broken Buddha fingers were preserved in the Dalai Lama's collection.

By all accounts, the Dalai Lama even gave the sculptor a bag of "oceans" that still contained the scent of the old days. Indeed, they were "oceans" from decades ago that had once rained in a downpour on the masses in Tibet. A Tibetan who fled to India had given them to the Dalai Lama as an offering. In turn, the Dalai Lama now planned to use them to remold the statue. Some said the bag of "oceans" melted into the thousand arms of the Avalokiteshvara that would help all living beings; others believed the bag of "oceans" was traded against Indian silver ingots used to construct the crystal-clear, beautiful body of the Avalokiteshvara statue.

At last, the sculptors had successfully completed the statues for the Avalokiteshvara, the Buddha, and the Guru Rinpoche. According to the Dalai Lama's records, "The thousand-armed and thousand-eyed Avalokiteshvara was built in 1970, the Tibetan year of the Iron Dog. The statue head contains three of the five ruined faces from Lhasa." Close to the models of the new statues, the two scarred faces were placed in the upper and lower layers of wooden boxes—surrounded and wrapped with packages of esoteric yellow *khatas*—a symbol of calamity and impermanence, yet suffused with an inexplicable sorrow. Above the box was a framed photo from the past of Lhasa's Tsuglagkhang, known to have been taken by the well-known aristocrat Tsarong Dasang Damdul, who was arrested after the occupation and died in prison in Lhasa in 1959. The frail photo showed three spectacular heads of the Avalokiteshvara that had not yet been destroyed: Adorned by priceless jewelry, it was astonishingly beautiful. Beneath it read two lines written in Tibetan: "Constructed in the time of the King of Tibet Songtsen Gampo and placed in the Jokhang Temple in Lhasa—the five-faced Avalokiteshvara."

Here's one more anecdote related to this grand Avalokiteshvara statue: It's about a sandalwood snake-hearted Goddess of Mercy statue originally placed in its heart. King Songtsen Gampo welcomed it from Nepal when constructing Tsuglagkhang. Later, his spirit was transformed into rays of light, which fused within, where it remained unstirred for over 1,300 years, until it was dumped by the Red Guards into the devastated pile of smattered Buddha statues. A devout Tibetan quietly picked it up and hid it in the dark. When the Dalai Lama received his Nobel Peace Prize in 1989, the Tibetan risked his life traveling through the snow mountains, and the statue

through various hands landed in Dharamsala as a gift for the Dalai Lama, rightfully and solely for his personal worship. During an interview in 1998 with American journalist Thomas Laird, the Dalai Lama showed him this lost and found sacred figure. In tears, his face glowed like a child's. The statue clearly meant much to the Dalai Lama, who even covered his nose so as not to exhale into it. "*Nying-je*," he exclaimed. "The first time I set eyes on this tiny wooden statue, I was overwhelmed with compassion."

In my second book of oral history about Tibet during the Cultural Revolution, *Memories of Tibet* (2006), I took down a story narrated by Choekyi,

an elderly woman who resides in the area of the Meru Neighborhood Committee:

> During the renovation of the Jokhang Temple in Dharamsala, whenever the workers were sculpting the *Thukje Chenpo*,[14] the Avalokiteshvara of a Thousand Arms and Eyes, something was always amiss, and they could never succeed. Thinking that it wasn't the right moment, they ended up letting it go. When the Cultural Revolution broke out in Tibet, the Jokhang's *Thukje Chenpo* was destroyed. As it turned out, the workers in

Dharamsala were reconstructing the Buddha statue and this time round, they succeeded in finishing the task. Later, after the Cultural Revolution, people from Tibet visited India and spoke of this incident, only to find out that it took place at the same time, as if the soul of the Avalokiteshvara had "traveled" from Chinese-ruled Tibet to the other Tibet in India.

No ending to this story is more fitting and marvelous, but nevertheless mingled with the bittersweet emotion of impermanence. I think of the old man who lived like a dog during the Cultural Revolution and lamented, "What's the point of living up to a ripe old age? I've even seen the death of a bodhisattva. What could be more distressing?" Still, the soul of a suffering bodhisattva lives on for an eternity; is this a metaphor for a reversal of fate, turning into a bodhisattva while one is still alive? It is said that after melting, the silver may not be pure enough, but I take side with the claim that it was silver coins that molded the statue of Avalokiteshvara. In my mind, I see flashbacks of silver coins from China and mud from India, and how devotees risked their lives smuggling ruined faces of a bodhisattva statue out from the lost Lhasa: Under what future circumstances might the spiritual meaning behind the resurrection of this Avalokiteshvara statue in a foreign land, facing toward Tibet day and night, be revealed one day? I was also told that during an important religious gathering, the Dalai Lama announced emotionally, "One day, when we exiled Tibetans can return to our homeland, this reborn *Thukje Chenpo* will also come home with us."

> January 2010, Beijing
> Revised—August 2016, Beijing

NOTES

1. Nyarong (the Tibetan name) is located in today's PRC administrative division of Sichuan Province, Kardze Tibetan Autonomous Prefecture, Nyarong County. [author's note]

2. From *Brandishing a Sword in Tibet* (2014), originally written in Japanese by Yang Haiying (1964–), a scholar of Mongolian studies based in Japan. [author's note]

3. *Pulu* is Tibetan for "wool." [author's note]

4. The Tibetan word *sar jie* (revolution) can also be rendered in Chinese characters as "killing" and "plundering."

5. The Norbulingka (Tibetan for "Jewel Garden") was built during the time of the Seventh Dalai Lama and has over three hundred years of history. It later became the summer palace of the Dalai Lamas. In the night of March 17, 1959, the fourteenth Dalai Lama started out on the road to exile. Under the gunfire of the Chinese Communist troops, many of the Tibetans who were defending the Dalai Lama were captured and killed. The Norbulingka has become a silent witness to one of the most significant changes in Tibetan history. [author's note]

6. See "Arriving at the Destination—The Tibetan Capital of Lhasa," accessed May 7, 2025, http://xxyylloo1.blog.qhnews.com/article/120-135.shtml (link no longer available). [author's note]

7. Woeser uses a wordplay on the words *delegates* and *watch-wearers*: In Chinese, they are pronounced the same way (*dai-biao-tuan*).

8. Yuan Shikai (1859–1916) was an influential political and military figure and a warlord during the late Manchu dynasty. After the 1911 revolution, which overthrew the last imperial dynasty of China, Yuan became the first president of the Republic of China. He attempted to reinstate himself as the emperor in 1916, but failed. [author's note]

9. Born in Yangzhou, Jiangsu Province, Tao Changsong volunteered to work as a Chinese-language teacher at a junior high school in Lhasa upon his graduation from East China Normal University in 1960. During the Cultural Revolution, he was the organizer and leader of the Red Guards, as well as the head of the rebel faction in Lhasa. He also served as the assistant chief of the Tibet Autonomous Region

(TAR) revolutionary committee before taking on a position at the TAR Tibetan Academy of of Social Sciences. Now retired, he still resides in Lhasa. [author's note]

10. The Tukje Lhakang is a chapel adjacent to the main hall in the Jokhang. The Jokhang is a complex made up of many chapels.

11. The statue has a history of more than 1,300 years, as documented from the time of King Songtsen Gampo, who had personally carried it to this sacred place. King Songtsen Gampo, recognized as the greatest king in Tibetan history, founded and unified the ancient Tubo dynasty [the Tibetan Empire] during the seventh century. Known for introducing Buddhism to Tibet, he also built the Potala Palace and established Lhasa as the capital of Tibet. [author's note]

12. *Zhungzhug* are objects hidden inside a Buddhist statue, such as gold and silver, elixirs, spices, grains, and others. They are considered sacred. The statue is not considered sacred unless it is filled with *zhungzhug*. [author's note]

13. "Kazara" is a term for Lhasa residents of mixed Nepalese and Tibetan heritage. The Kazara enjoy a special resident status in Lhasa despite being citizens of Nepal. [author's note]

14. *Thukje Chenpo* means "Great Compassion" in Tibetan.

13

Remembering a Smashed Buddha

Twenty days since Lhasa.
I still think of that smashed Buddha face.
On a little vendor stand in front of Tromsikhang community center.
I could see it from afar.
I'd wanted to buy some *droma* from the Tromsikhang Market,[1]
but sorrow struck when I saw it.
I couldn't help but approach its battered state,
feel its life, as it leaned painfully on a shelf,
face smashed, arms amputated, its body chopped off at the waist.
It leaned so painfully on a shelf.
Soy sauce, bean paste, salad dressing, and rolls of toilet paper surrounded it:
All entered our life from China long ago.
A colored stone pendant, once exquisite, hung on its neck,
its chest bore a strange sphinx.
Sitting together on a ruined pagoda.
Which sacred monastery or pious home once venerated them?
It leaned painfully on a shelf.
Even though it looked calm like still waters, pain jabbed itself into my bones.
I looked at it sadly, like watching a story,
the past and the present of a story.
Ah, I could feel the misty fate that brought us together,
like melted snow seeping into me from high mountain peaks.
The vendor hugged his knees
and touted, *Come on, buy! An old Buddha, isn't it great?*
When did it get smashed like this? I asked.
Cultural Revolution. He looked up. *Of course it's the Cultural Revolution.*
How much? I wanted to buy it, to bring it home,
but this vendor from Jiangxi insisted, *Three thousand yuan.*
With reluctance and regret,
I left that smashed Buddha.
Just took some pictures.

So whenever I think back, I can turn on my computer and see it.
Friends say it could be a brand-new Buddha, deliberately smashed
      to fetch a better price,
who knows, its Cultural Revolution past was just an invention.
Yes, who knows, but the pain is still there.
I write these lines to let go.

     May 14, 2007—Beijing

NOTE

   1. *Droma* refers to the Tibetan yam.

14

The Ruins of Lhasa

Yabzhi Taktser

There are two Chinese transliterations for the term *Yabzhi*, "Yaxi" and "Yaoxi." In the Tibetan language, *Yab* is the highest honorific term for father, whereas *zhi* refers to a clan's residence. All Tibetans know the word and what it means. According to Tibetan tradition, and in line with scholarly research, "*Yabzhi* [*yab-gzhis*] refers to the families of former Dalai Lamas," to quote the renowned Italian Tibetologist Luciano Petech. Official Chinese Tibetologists too claim that "people use the word *Yabzhi* (the father's residence) that signifies both power and wealth to pay homage to the families of Dalai Lamas, which is why *Yabzhi* has become a commonly recognized and oft-used noun." For lack of a better definition, one should translate *Yabzhi* as "the residence of the nation's founding father."

Like most Tibetans, I've always believed that Tibet has had many different Dalai Lamas and as such, there should also be many different *Yabzhi* families. But scholars affirm, "Today, there are six *Yabzhi* families, including the current Dalai Lama's," namely Sangpo the family of the Seventh Dalai Lama, Lhalu the families of the Eighth and Twelfth Dalai Lamas, Yuthok the family of the Tenth Dalai Lama, Phunkhang the family of the Eleventh Dalai Lama, Langdun the family of the Thirteenth Dalai Lama, and, last but not least, Taktser the family of the current Fourteenth Dalai Lama. His Holiness comes from Taktser in Amdo, which, according to the current Chinese administrative divisions, is Hongya Village in Ping'an County, Qinghai Province. This is to say that the title *Yabzhi* contains a specific history. Truth is, I don't know why I've decided to elaborate about this, but I've met so many *Yabzhi* families that it seems many wouldn't hesitate to randomly or freely add the *Yabzhi* title before their family names—all just for a touch of nobility, glory, and glamour.

As mentioned earlier, I've encountered countless "*Yabzhi* X" and "*Yabzhi* Y." Take, for example, the family of Phagpala Gelek Namgyal from Chamdo:[1] Even his elder brother, who once held a Chinese government post, has now added *Yabzhi* to his last name. It must have been some post–Cultural Revolution "fashion." Prior to these times, who would have even dared to openly call himself *Yabzhi*? In fact, it was considered part of the "Four Olds" swept into the dustbin of history: Even genuine aristocratic families wished then that they were blacksmiths or butchers instead; some hastily "married down" or associated themselves with "lowly people" whose shadows they would have otherwise shunned.

But what goes around comes around: In just twenty or thirty years, things have completely changed. Today many Tibetans dream of becoming aristocrats overnight. To do so, they spare no efforts to fabricate stories that portray themselves as relatives of the most powerful, or as princes and princesses. This, to the extent that descendants of the Rinpoches—who passed on their monastic traditions from generation to generation, but were compelled to return to secular life during those so-called abnormal times—first found themselves inheriting such tumultuous history:[2] As pitiful "products" of a muddled epoch, with no reason to feel pride, but also conferring upon themselves the title *Yabzhi* out of the blue.

All *Yabzhi* in the world are but one huge family. Does this mean that all these new, self-created "*Yabzhi* clans" are now bonded by blood?

What about the genuine *Yabzhi* families?

What remains in Lhasa of Tenzin Gyatso, our current Fourteenth Dalai Lama's family?

Let's take a look at a photograph, probably taken before 1959.

I see a spacious white building, grand and august at the heart of a vast tree-lined compound or garden. It is located between Lhasa's old town and the Potala Palace. One can spot it when looking down to the left from the top floor of the palace. This is none other than the Dalai Lama's official family residence: Yabzhi Taktser Residence, otherwise known as Yabzhi Taktser. It's also called Changseshar. From reliable records we learn that this residence was not adjacent to other aristocratic residences. It was "the only stand-alone residence" in Lhasa's old town, within the Lingkor, the area of the longest circumambulation. It was built right where it now stands such that whenever the Dalai Lama, living high up in the Potala Palace, missed his home and family, all he needed to do was look to the left and see from

afar the silhouettes of his siblings, and perhaps even smell the fragrance of his favorite Amdo bread baked by his mother.

In her autobiography (later published in Taiwan), *Dalai Lama, My Son: A Mother's Story* (1997),[3] the Fourteenth Dalai Lama's mother, Diki Tsering, explains that *Changse* means "under the majestic sight of the Dalai Lama," whereas *shar* refers to "the eastern side of the Potala Palace." Such a poetic name calls attention to the noble yet humane character of Lhasa's aristocrats, who helped to source the location for the young Dalai Lama and his family when they had just arrived from the border region. The construction of this special residence near the Potala Palace began in 1939, when the four-year-old Dalai Lama was invited to Lhasa. It was completed in around 1941. Alas, the place was under "the majestic sight of the Dalai Lama" for only a little over two decades. In the night of March 17, 1959, when the Dalai Lama, at age twenty-four, quietly left the occupied city of Lhasa to embark on his long exile, his family too lost their home. As His Holiness's mother recalls:

> Originally, this piece of land belonged to the Thirteenth Dalai Lama. The British Legation was interested in purchasing it, but the Thirteenth Dalai Lama refused, insisting that it might be useful to him or his people at some point. It was a vast space full of trees and nature.

We stayed three years at Norbulingka before moving to this new home...Our Tibetan government had sent someone to inform us that our new house was ready.

It *was* our home. The government invited lamas to bless the place. Four lamas stayed on with us permanently. On every eighth day, we would pray and give our offerings. From time to time we invited fifty to a hundred lamas to join us for a weeklong group prayer.

Our residence Changseshar was built of stone and had three stories and pillars. It was constructed by the Tibetan government. A two-story house was added beyond the courtyard.

I gave birth to two of my sons at Changseshar. The son who lived on to adulthood was named Tenzin Choegyal; he was born in 1946. My other son Tenzin Chodak died at two. He was so lively and adorable. He often ran into His Holiness's chambers and made a mess out of everything. He died from a bronchial infection that lasted several months. At his death, we invited the Gadong oracle to do a divination...In a trance the Gadong oracle assured us that our dead son would somehow return to us.

Before his first long journey to China, we invited His Holiness over for a few days at Changseshar. He'd never been to our home, so it was a great honor—for me and for our entire household. We had to prepare food for His Holiness as well as for his retinue of government officials and those awaiting to seek an audience with him. It was a heavy responsibility. Prayers were held daily prior to his departure for China. The entire *Kashag*, the Cabinet, was present, so were several aristocrats. We built a new kitchen before he arrived, and a new driveway too, for his car to drive right up to the house.

In her autobiography, I noticed two photographs of His Holiness's mother standing on the rooftop of Changseshar. They were taken during Losar, the Tibetan New Year. She was dressed in a *chuba*, though the colorful brocades on her shoulders indicated that hers was no traditional *chuba* but one from Amdo. Other than earrings, she wore no jewelry. How simple yet stylish.

After her husband's death, as she writes, she'd put on her Amdo brocades only for very special occasions. In the second photo, she was holding in her arms the young Ngari Rinpoche dressed in a robe. Ngari Rinpoche was only a young boy when he followed His Holiness into exile. I've also come across a photo of His Holiness's mother with her three sons, and behind them a traditional Tibetan-style door-hanging, but I've no idea if this was a door to Changseshar.

After the Chinese army invaded Lhasa in 1950, nothing was the same. Of their early years, His Holiness's mother recalls, "The Chinese came to Changseshar and told me it would be a good idea to convert the residence into state government offices. They wanted to pay me cash. I refused. They threatened that if I wouldn't accept their money, people would accuse them of robbing me . . . They dropped in anytime they wanted. Whenever they informed me of their 'visit,' I grew nervous, wondering what they exactly had in mind to discuss with me. When they left, I felt an inexpressible lightness and heaved a sigh of relief. I was so afraid. I had to be very careful of what I said, for fear of reckless words that might bring harm to someone else."

Diki Tsering distinctly recalls the day when they had to leave Changseshar: March 12, 1959. Although the Tibetan resistance against the Chinese government was underway, Diki Tsering was oblivious. She was at home embroidering, in the midst of her house chores. All seemed tranquil within Changseshar, while at the foot of Potala Palace thousands of women were

shouting slogans to protect the Dalai Lama. Eventually her son-in-law, who served as His Holiness's chief bodyguard, came by the residence to fetch her for Norbulingka:

> I'd never imagined that was the last I would ever see of Changseshar and my own mother. I didn't even have time to pack anything. We just left for India.
>
> All my possessions were locked in Changseshar. I wrapped up the keys with silk, leaving them behind with a note for my *chang-zo*, our house-keeper . . . I told him to take charge of the house and that I was placing the keys in his custody . . . I didn't even have time to bid my mother farewell.

Already eighty-seven, His Holiness's grandmother could not travel on horseback. Left with no choice but to stay behind, she died a lonely death two years later in Lhasa during its upheaval.

Decades later, when I could finally visit Changseshar, I failed to find a trace that remotely reminded us of its idyllic past. Instead, I was confronted with a drastically disparate scene: signs describing Changseshar as "the second guesthouse" of the Tibet Autonomous Region government or signboards that read "Headquarters of the Rebel Faction," referring implicitly to one of Lhasa's main rebel bases, where Red Guards from all across China during the Cultural Revolution were based before they went about destroying the sacred city. Changseshar had been converted into a hotel, the rooms inhabited by its maintenance staff and of course, the paying guests. The place had turned into a chaotic, decrepit compound, where everyone was only inter-

ested in minding their own business. Today, a black signboard in both Tibetan and Chinese, LHASA PRESERVED HISTORICAL AND CULTURAL SITE YABZHI TAKTSER, is erected on the entrance wall. Its address, as indicated online: No. 31, Beijing Middle Road, Lhasa Chengguang District.

I think Yabzhi Taktser is without dispute one of Lhasa's most prominent landmarks. Its heritage is just as significant as any other historic building's. Sadly, few people know about it. That may well be a blessing in disguise, after all. Otherwise, it might suffer a global invasion by tourists. Speaking of which, Changseshar has indeed been rather lucky. Despite its run-down state and its continual decomposition, it seems unlikely to collapse anytime soon. Close to two-thirds of the compound remains intact at the original site. Undeniably, the Dalai Lama's family escaped to India and the place was robbed of its aura and presence by Communist "liberators." It was the metaphorical equivalent of the "green upstarts" in Vladimir Nabokov's narrative of exile, in which the Russian writer reimagines his home and past as he "now hide[s] the second-floor east-corner window of the room where [he] was born."[4] Appropriated by the revolution, Yabzhi Taktser has, for years, served as a shelter for people from all trades. If you ask any passerby today, no one can tell you that this used to be the royal residence of His Holiness's family. They will indicate matter-of-factly that it is an annex of the Tibetan Mansion or, more conveniently, the Tibetan Pearl Garden Hotel.

Last summer, a Tibetan netizen who identified himself by the screen name "Snowland Dust" posted sixteen photos on his blog, revealing the interior and exterior architecture of Yabzhi Taktser. Given that the buildings in these pictures appear less ruined than they are now, I reckon they must have been photographed over a decade ago. Heads of the infamous family of Communist monsters—Marx, Engels, Lenin, Stalin, and Mao—drawn onto the inner wall are nonetheless discernible.

Next to his photographs (now vanished from the virtual space along with their blog post), the netizen "Snowland Dust" inserted an edifying introductory paragraph:

> After several long negotiations between the Tibetan government and the Dalai Lama's parents (in particular his father), they decided to build this residence about five hundred meters to the east of Potala Palace. The building dates back roughly to the time between 1939 and 1941 . . . It occupies an approximate area of 3,500 square meters with an estimated floor area of 2,700 square meters. It was erected in traditional Tibetan style, without any exceptional or modern components. The entire compound is separated into two main parts, the inner and outer courtyards. The two-story high outer yard was mainly used by servants and official personnel accompanying the Dalai Lama. The three-story high inner courtyard functioned as a gathering place for the Dalai Lama and other important officials. The whole place encompasses roughly a hundred large and small rooms (including storage rooms). It's located at Beijing Middle Road, the most flourishing commercial street in present-day Lhasa, overshadowed

by the surrounding shops on the street. Not many know that this was once the residence of the Dalai Lama's parents.

Needless to say, this mysterious netizen is quite well informed about the inside details of Yabzhi Taktser. He summarizes:

Here are three main reasons why certain historical or cultural sites and aristocratic manors were not completely destroyed during the turmoil of the Cultural Revolution: First, they were used by the military; second, they served as offices or guesthouses for the government; third, they functioned as storerooms for the People's Communes or as a location for collective activities. The Dalai Lama's manor has survived because it was "recycled" into a state guesthouse: Its new name was simply the Second Government Guesthouse.

In 1964, Yabzhi Taktser was confiscated by the Chinese government and used as a guesthouse until 1990. It played a vital role as a major social address for state officials of all ranks, more so in times when the

公　　告
市级文物，请勿参观
拍照，谢谢合作！

The cultural relics of cit
y please don't visit and take
photo,thank for cooperation!

Chinese economy was relatively less developed than now. In 1990, the local government built a new and modern hotel, the Tibetan Mansion, which became a semicommercial state-run hotel. The Second Government Guesthouse (formerly the residence of the Dalai Lama's parents) was thus merged with this Tibetan Mansion. Between 1990 and 2005, rooms were rented out to hotel staff members, mainly Chinese workers. Around the courtyard they built commercial houses collectively known as the Tibetan Mansion's Department for Economic Development. To this day, these "houses" continue to generate revenue. Until 2011, the usage, rent, and commercial activities in these buildings have generated an estimated total of sixty-six million yuan.

The interior of the original building has since gone through striking modifications. To maximize rent, its main hall was split into two. Moreover, several offices were built for staff members managing tenants and collecting rent. Wall paintings in most rooms have been wiped off—that must have happened when the place was used as state-run guesthouse. This is also the case for the main scripture hall and the Dalai Lama's chamber where most elaborate murals and colored carvings are now erased. Portraits of Mao, Stalin, and others linger on the interior wall.

In conclusion the netizen reports without affect,

Since 1959, Yabzhi Taktser has never once been renovated. Out of the sixty-six million yuan generated as revenue, the government has not spent a single yuan on its upkeep. The main building of the residence is severely damaged, so no one has lived there since 2005. The whole complex is on the brink of falling apart. The outer main wall has collapsed in several spots. Water seeping through the roof for years has resulted in serious erosion and damage to the interior wooden structures and walls.

Why would the Chinese government not renovate or preserve the former residence of the Dalai Lama's parents, if not for the fact that they hate his politics? In name, the residence is listed as part of the municipal heritage conservation. In truth, anything related to the Dalai Lama is regarded as a political question, so how else would any department or rational individual find courage to engage in its preservation? Still, who knows: The residence might soon undergo renovation in hope of serving the United Front Work Department.

I've no recollection of my first visit to Yabzhi Taktser. In February 2003, I took a trip there to take some pictures for my book *Forbidden Memory: Tibet During the Cultural Revolution* (2006). It was a mild but sunny winter day. Looking at those photographs now, the place appeared less cluttered. Even the Ganden Phodrang, the Dalai Lama's residence at Potala, felt close within reach. Solar stoves with steaming water were spread out in the outer

yard. The main complex facing the sun was hung with clothes and quilts. I was using negative films and couldn't afford more than four or five pictures. What a pity that I didn't spend time around the inner yard.

In the summer of 2007, a shrewd businessman from Kham took my husband and me to Yabzhi Taktser. I prefer not to go into details about its changes since: Migrant traders enclosed the building like ants, conducting all sorts of business; the new buildings barely conformed to the authentic architecture, yet had taken up nearly the whole space. Back then I gave my word not to mention this in public, but let me say this now: This "businessman" from Kham was a kind soul who almost always deliberately concealed his good deeds. He wanted to do everything he could to restore the shabby Yabzhi Changseshar. Sadly, this will remain nothing but a wish. The "businessman" has since been framed and put behind bars.

These days, the exquisite old garden next to Lhasa River has been developed into the so-called "Xianzu Island" and is home to a massive "Xianzu Island Resort" comprising a flashy row of enclosed Tibetan-style buildings à la Changseshar. Apparently, Tibetan architects and designers were specially hired to model this complex on Changseshar. Despite its commercial agenda, it seeks to offer younger generations a glimpse into the pomp of the actual residence.

On the other hand, the once remarkable and respected white mansion is gradually vanishing. One barely finds it, not even from a height atop the Potala Palace. Far too many ugly high buildings in its vicinity have now engulfed the once lush and elegant garden area. I returned in the autumn of 2012 but found severe-looking guards in uniform stationed at the entrance gate. I took a longer route around the compound, horrified by its disrepair and neglect. Although metal scaffolding was constructed along its ruined walls, no renovation had ever begun. A year later, I was fortunate to have a chance to enter the Yabzhi Taktser ruins clandestinely. Walls were plastered with signboards of Sichuanese restaurants, public showers, and hairdressers. Standing right next to it was a new gigantic department store. I walked up to its fourth and fifth floors for a good overview of the sprawling ruins from a side stairway. Next to the majestic, brightly lit Potala Palace, dramatically overspread with Chinese flags, Yabzhi Taktser seemed ill and destitute.

As in a story in search of an ending, I chanced by Lhasa in 2014, this time with an artist friend from Beijing. Together we headed for Yabzhi Taktser. The front door was now bolted, and with a guard on duty, we could no longer enter the site. It was closed forever to the public. I understood that Yabzhi Taktser, like the monastic college Shideling and other ruins in Lhasa,

were scars of the violence inflicted on the city and its people. Although these ruins might disappear someday, their traces and absence live on like ghosts in the bodies of those alive.

Back in 2013 when I'd managed to enter Yabzhi Taktser, the vast courtyard was crowded with weeds. Along a stone path leading to the main chamber, sparse bicycles and motorbikes were parked as if the former mansion were now an industrial storage plant. Buildings on both sides were all two stories high. Four, five massive Tibetan mastiffs were barking ferociously on the ground floor. If the iron gates had been unlocked, we'd have been torn to pieces. I was trembling with fear when I took my GoPro camera and reached through the iron grid. One of the dogs jumped and snatched at the camera, as though it wanted to devour it. A Chinese trader next door came in to feed the dogs. Clearly, he had kept them as "commodities" to be put on sale someday. How hilarious: He who spoke only the Sichuan dialect summoned a Tibetan security guard to kick us out. In Tibetan I snapped back at him, "Tell me, who really owns this place?" Caught in his embarrassment, the Tibetan guard stared at me, bewildered and speechless.

Upstairs in the main complex that now resembled and smelt like an enormous rubbish dump, a corridor was crumbling. Railings made from imported Indian metal were rusty but stable. Shadows of alien decorations intrigued me. I entered the dusty dark rooms, some with walls plastered in posters of Chinese celebrities of the 1980s or newspaper cuttings from *Tibet Daily* during the 1990s. On doors I found a large, red Chinese character 福 [*fu*, fortune] or portraits of the mighty door deities. On others I found deathly pale seals that read SEALED ON JANUARY 7, 2005.

I walked from one room to the next, as if searching for something specific, and ended up taking tons of photos. One camera didn't suffice: I had two or three, not to mention my camera phone. Like eyes, their lenses peered into every nook and corner. But what was I seeking?

There was not a trace of life. Only signs of a previous life that still felt raw. Like in a thriller film, I secretly hoped to retrieve traces of that fateful night—March 17, 1959—when His Holiness and his family left their home behind. Yet the single fragile trace of life I could find in these ruins was also dead: a lifeless spider hanging midair in its web. Like the last surviving "patron" of this space, it protected the ruins and its past. What was trapped in its web? What about other spiders? Were they also protecting the ruins?

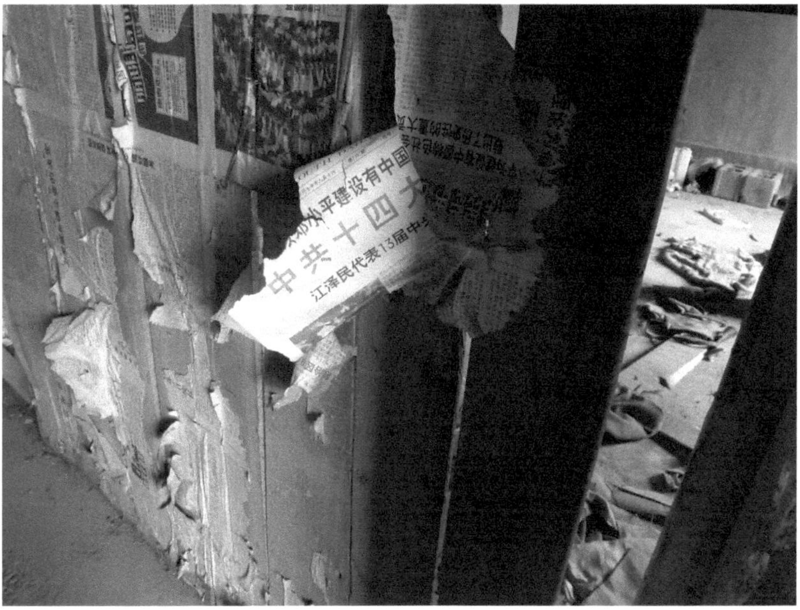
平建设有中国
中共十四大
江泽民代表13届中

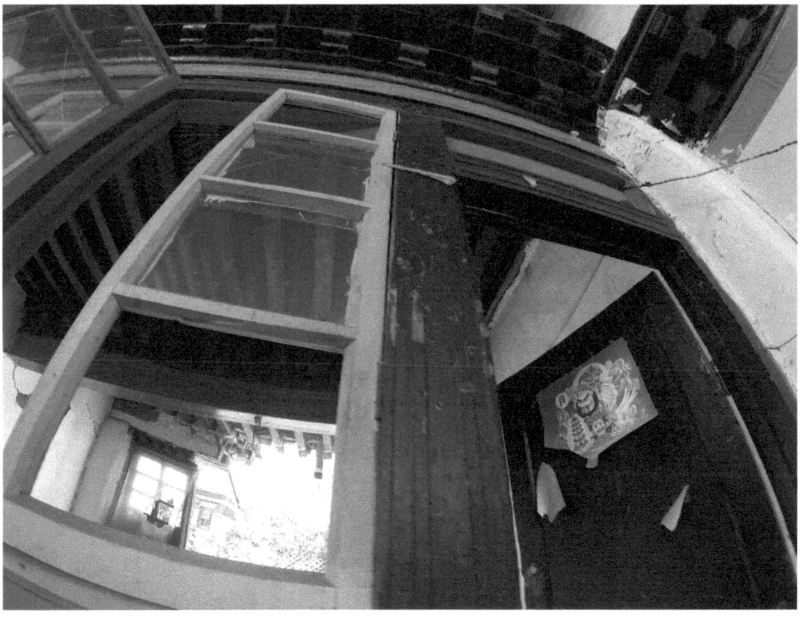

I'm curious about spiders: How does our culture view them as creatures? Do these animals embody metaphorical meaning or power? Are they malicious? Do they drive out the evil? I took a close-up shot of the hanging spider: its corpse against a surreal, dilapidated setting, as though an untold tale was hidden deeper somewhere. Back in the old times, there must have been more animals than spiders living in this mansion. The household no doubt had cats, rats, and dogs—in particular the Apso, a special Lhasa dog—and they were probably allowed in the main hall, living room, or even bedrooms. Side by side with guards in the courtyard or at the main gate, dogs such as the huge Tibetan mastiffs kept watch. In those photographs of the Dalai Lama during the 1960s, I've seen several Apso dogs. Apparently, they too had followed him into exile. Spiders, on the other hand, seemed much more resilient than cats or dogs: Spiders could easily hide and therefore easily survive.

What struck me as most poignant, however, was not the Potala Palace viewed against the backlight out the shattered window. Nor was it the devastating corridors and rooms on the third floor. It was a mirror affixed to a pillar in the deserted main hall. I had to stay away from it; how else would I recover fleeting traces and critical moments from that fatal night in 1959? Wasn't that the resonant voice of His Holiness who spoke with pain from his exile, "Your home, your country and friends have suddenly vanished"? I thought of Russian poet Joseph Brodsky, who muses in his poem "Torso," "This is the end of things. This is, at the road's end, / a mirror by which to enter."[5] Yet when one enters, "the ages vanish round the bend," only to find oneself as a reflection in the mirror: alone, helpless yet so mesmerizing, as though forever hiding in the mirror, never to be stalked, threatened, or humiliated by the state apparatus again.

I took a photo of myself standing in front of the broken mirror. In the picture, I was in fact the reflection of a spirit present in the room. The one in the mirror did and did not resemble me: It took after someone who lived here years back. Such alienating effects, coupled with an eerie attachment and intimacy, almost made my eyes water. Might I in an earlier life have also taken a picture in front of this mirror before discreetly entering a third dimension to participate in one of history's major upheavals?

In another room, I found an old object: a wooden block that must have dropped from somewhere. It was so richly detailed and delicately carved that it came across as a miniature of this old mansion. I decided to take it home with me.

What and who am I?

A covert amateur archaeologist?

A woman obsessed with collecting remnants from the past?

Or am I just another exiled Tibetan who found herself back in this old town, cherishing past memories and lives?

Pacing among these ruins, I was transported to their past, as if traveling on a misty road lured by the exotic, flickering sunlight. Alive once again in these ruins, I couldn't help but feel protected and content.

This is how I feel about Lhasa and its ruins after all these years. No matter how I see and observe the physical ruins, I am blind to the spiritual ruins. In his autobiographical essay "Less Than One," Brodsky writes, "You cannot cover a ruin with a page of *Pravda*. The empty windows gaped at us like skulls' orbits, and as little as we were, we sensed tragedy. True, we couldn't connect ourselves to the ruins, but that wasn't necessary: They emanated enough to interrupt laughter."[6] I'm afraid the "curse of oblivion" will take effect only upon the ultimate disappearance of these ruins. To echo contemporary Chinese art critic Liao Wen, who left me this message on WeChat: *When power lands in the hands of ignorance or materialism, any culture and aesthetics will be deprived of their soul.* Tragically, the Chinese authorities are the ones imbued with the power of casting the "curse of oblivion" on us.

I've evoked and written about ruins in more than ten of my books. Besides writing, I enjoy using my "ruins photographs" to contextualize Lhasa's history and geography since its suppression—and consequently, invisibility—under Chinese occupation. Ruins personify a city within a city, a people within a people, a death among death. Much resides within the ruins. I focus on their seemingly trivial details: flowers blossoming in the vast courtyard, a dead spider hanging in midair while the main building is slowly disintegrating, the remains of newspaper cuttings from *Tibet Daily*, torn posters, an old mirror affixed to a pillar, or the flooring once made from highland Aga soil, no doubt more durable than our ceramic tiles today . . . Weeds and plants struggle through the clay surface. By the grace of these details, I've come to accept the inexplicable.

Far from being a professional photographer, I follow my heart and equip myself with whatever tools I can find or afford: film cameras, digital cameras (normal and digital SLR), GoPro, and, for better or worse, my cell phone. I must confess that photographing using GoPro and cell phones turns out to be rather addictive; you can take thousands of photos in one go. I've produced extensive images that serve as visual chronicles of these ruins. In time, they will come to be valued documentation about distinct areas in our vanishing Lhasa. I like to imagine that each element or shadow captured in my pictures contains a secret code to Lhasa and Tibet. As with artists at the turn of last century who preserved the old Baudelairean Paris in prints and images, Lhasa is the museum whose history, ambiance, impressions, and testimony I hope to photograph and save for the future.

One more story—

The narrator is a retired cadre whom I met on my journey to Lhasa. She ridiculed herself for having once worked as "the Dalai Lama's slave." In truth, she was a live-in servant. The Communist Party labels these live-in servants as "slaves" even though they were technically "vassals." I'd presumed that she would condemn the past and sing praises of the present as others would, but little did I expect her generous words: "People like to deceive themselves into thinking that the Tibetans are now blessed with happiness after their harsh suffering during the Dalai Lama's rule, but those like us who've known the past know the truth."

She continued, "Yes, my family used to be slaves of the Dalai Lama, if you must insist that we were slaves. My father was a guard at Yabzhi Taktser. I grew up in Yabzhi Taktser with Kundun's sister Jetsun Pema and his older sister's daughter Khando La.[7] We used to play together every day. Sometimes we went crazy in the garden; Khando La would have us hide behind trees, as she knew Kundun often looked at us from the Potala Palace with his binoculars. We were so happy. On the contrary, Kundun had never experienced such joy as a child. Once, Khando La urged me to wade through a pond. I refused, so she hit me mischievously. I wept and snitched on her. In the end, Kundun's mother told her off, and Khando La even had to seek my father for help so I would play with her again.

"Kundun's mother was a benevolent woman who lavished us, the servants' children, with fruit. As you know, fruit was rare back then. Rooms in the courtyards were saved for strangers, vagrants, and pilgrims who worked in return for butter, tsampa, and meat. Kundun's mother never stopped giving them food.

"I've never met Kundun's father, though I heard of his bad temper and honesty. He liked horses and spent most of his time in the stable.

"Once I ended up with a bleeding scar on my face. To alleviate the pain, I sat in the courtyard and exposed the wound to the sun. Kundun's third brother Losang Samten La was returning on his horseback when he saw me suffer. Quickly he sent someone to fetch me butter tea, tea drunk by Kundun himself. I smeared some on my face, stayed a little longer, and, true enough, just after a few days the wound healed.

"Many servants were living in Changseshar. When one of them died, Kundun's family took care of his son."

Soon seventy, the retired cadre bore wrinkles over her face but showed signs of youth and exuberance whenever she laughed. She'd since visited Dharamsala and sought an audience with the Dalai Lama. Speaking of His Holiness, now that he must live in a foreign land, she shed tears. Like most Tibetans, she evoked her immense gratitude to India. There she too reunited with her childhood playmate Jetsun Pema. Before we parted ways, she reminded me, "Once our masters, forever our masters. Never forget that we're our own masters."

I smiled. How affectionately she uttered the word "master,"[8] as if we were speaking of one big family.

September 2015, Beijing
Revised—June 2016

1. Phagpala Gelek Namgyal (1940–) was a prominent figure when China was taking over. He is a lama and government official.

2. Rinpoches are revered reincarnations of spiritual teachers and lamas.

3. An English edition was published by Compass Books (Penguin) in 2000.

4. Vladimir Nabokov, *Speak, Memory: An Autobiography Revised* (New York: Vintage International, 1989), 18. See also Svetlana Boym, "Vladimir Nabokov's False Passport," in *The Future of Nostalgia* (New York: Basic Books, 2002), 263.

5. Joseph Brodsky, "Torso," in *Collected Poems in English* (New York: Farrar, Straus and Giroux, 2000), 78.

6. Joseph Brodsky, "Less Than One," in *Less Than One: Selected Essays* (New York: Farrar, Straus and Giroux, 1986), 27.

7. "Kundun" is a respectful title used for the Dalai Lama. The literal meaning of the Tibetan word is "presence."

8. The Tibetan word for "master" is *dagbo*.

15

Let Me Write, the Fear of Lhasa Breaks My Heart

Dashing off a goodbye to Lhasa—
now a city of fear.

Dashing off a goodbye to Lhasa—
where fears outgrow all the fears from 1959, 1969, and 1989.[1]

Dashing off a goodbye to Lhasa—
whose fear is in your breath and heartbeat. Choked within the silence
and the words you wish to say.

Dashing off a goodbye to Lhasa—
where fear is wrought by countless gunned soldiers, policemen, and
plainclothes agents. Wrought even more by the massive state
machine. Never aim at them, they'll point a gun at you, or take
you away to an unknown corner.

Dashing off a goodbye to Lhasa—
where fear begins at the Potala and grows east. It spreads to the
Tibetan district, where eerie footsteps echo without their
shadows, even more horrifying than invisible ghosts in daylight.
A few times, I brushed past the cold guns in their hands.

Dashing off a goodbye to Lhasa—
where fear is scrutinized by every camera in every street, office,
temple hall, and monastery. Prying into every mind from the
outside. *Take care. They're watching us*, whisper the Tibetans who
say no more.

Dashing off a goodbye to Lhasa—
whose fear breaks my heart. Let me write!

[You have guns, I have a pen.]

August 23, 2008—leaving Lhasa

NOTE

1. They refer to the 1959 Communist invasion of Tibet, the June 1969 repression of the Tibetan revolt during the Cultural Revolution in Nyemo, and the March 1989 repression of the Tibetan demonstrations in Lhasa.

16

Only This Useless Poem
—for Lobsang Tsepak

Lobsang Tsepak, a monk aged twenty-six from the Kirti Monastery in Ng-aba, Sichuan Province, was a student at the Central University for Ethnic Nationalities in Beijing. Arrested on March 25, 2011, for ambiguous reasons, he was alleged to have disclosed details about the Tibetan monk Phuntsog's self-immolation to the public outside Tibet.

1

Already the twenty-third day
Reading a poem, "Disappeared"
I think of you right away

You disappeared one afternoon last month, on the 25th
I can do nothing but cry and write poems

2

Like cinema requiring scenery shots
my thoughts in chaos
flash images of reverie
Flowers trampled by horses, black tents in the pastures
prayer flags in a breeze, birds and beasts now set free
I've seen such beautiful scenery at home
In reality, in such difficult times
you seem to have evaporated

3

Absurdity is reality
I've become my own poison
you, a sacrificial offering that tasted poison

All I see is you when I close my eyes
That March, flames spread in the Land of Snows
Compatriots carried bleeding protestors to the monastery
worshipping them in the temple of their hearts

4
March is the cruelest month
said a scholarly foreign journalist
who visited Tibet in two Marches. Perhaps he saw something
or nothing
Obviously he'd fallen into the traps of the thirty-six stratagems
Did you say that the Tibetans howled like wolves?
Sheepishly he looked ashamed

5
Brother Tsepak, where are you?
Were you brutally sent back to Ngaba?
Or locked and tortured in a dark room?

I heard from a brother how he was tortured to confession
hung upside-down, with three ribs broken
When it turned cold, he cringed in pain . . .
Sigh, I forgot to ask him, where it just snowed in the east, is he now
    safe and well?
But who can I ask for Brother Tsepak's whereabouts?

6
Our lives no longer feel ground under them
At ten paces you can't hear our words . . .
This is a verse by a poet of conscience who died under Stalin[1]
also a portrayal of China at its height

Late at night, I rambled
I don't know if it'd be useful, but I'll still speak out
In fact I know, it's useless even if I do speak out . . .

A friend from a free country replied firmly
They always want to make you think that speaking out is useless
But we must not stop speaking out!

7

Both hands empty
my right hand grabs a pen, the left holds memories
Although memories now yield to the pen
tears run ceaseless between the lines
a trampled dignity

8

If you gaze at hell for too long
you risk being eaten bit by bit

Are you willing to negotiate?
If so, we'll listen
in exchange for his safe return

Suddenly I remember a spooky afternoon
a spooky falcon and hound who yelled fiercely

You, can't you not write about Tibet?

9

If I don't write about Tibet, there won't be poems

If not for Tibet, Brother Tsepak
would not disappear
If not for Tibet, Brothers Tapey and Phuntsog
would not self-immolate

This list of names can be very long, very long . . .

But this Tibet
its name means the Hidden West

> April 4, 2011—Beijing
> Finalized—April 17, 2011

NOTE

1. "A poet of conscience" refers to Osip Mandelstam (1891–1938), a Russian
poet from the Silver Age. After reciting to friends an epigram that denounced Stalin, Mandelstam was arrested in 1934 and exiled. After returning from Voronezh
in 1937, he was arrested for "counterrevolutionary" activities in May 1938 and sentenced to five years in a labor camp. He attempted suicide on several occasions and
died in the Gulag Archipelago on December 27, 1938.

17

Back to Lhasa, Day One

from *Seven Days in Lhasa*

Monday, August 17, 2008

This is not a diary.

Three days before the Olympics, I left Beijing with my husband Wang Li-xiong [hereafter referred to as W]. The capital city was no longer its usual self. When we arrived at a house near a Tibetan monastery in Amdo, the opening ceremony had illuminated the skies of Beijing with rounds of fireworks that blurred day and night. I was far from being in high spirits. A Rinpoche sat next to us and started chatting. Looking at the TV without watching it, he tried to tell us how dramatically Tibetan life had changed. As he struggled to speak in standard Tibetan, I was amused listening to his Amdo accent.

The Beijing Olympics did not mean anything to us—how remote they were from our realities—yet deep in our hearts, we were mindful of how all that had happened earlier this year related to this much anticipated international event. Several times the Rinpoche couldn't resist turning the volume down to stop the hysterical yells on his TV. To mask my sadness, I drank cup after cup of milk tea.

The next day, we headed for a monastery where time had stopped in March. Two monks showed me the deep wounds from wires tied around their wrists and lamented aloud what we knew all along, *The world has forgotten the call of Tibet and the plight of Tibetans . . .*

My narrative begins the night before August 17.

The five of us set out in a Korean four-wheel drive along the Qinghai–Tibet Highway toward a bend entering Nagchu. We felt as if we were setting foot in hell. It was pitch-black and drizzling. Only scant lights from houses scattered over the landscape were visible from afar. I held on to my registration card for speed limits, a piece of paper with the following characters printed in ink: COMPLY WITH REGULATIONS. Technical phrases such as CAR NUMBER PLATE, CAR MODEL, SPEED LIMIT, DESTINATION, and ESTIMATED TIME OF ARRIVAL appeared in both Tibetan and Chinese. If I remember correctly, the preventive measure was implemented in 2007. With over 4 million tourists visiting Tibet, the autonomous region suffered from a high number of car accidents. The regional authorities resorted to imposing all manner of administrative measures on speed limits in an attempt to curb the rise in car accidents. But tourism had declined sharply this year, so the policy must have been meant for something else. Surveillance, perhaps?

I was struck by how Tibetan policemen at the checkpoint randomly reset our speed limit once they overheard me speak in Tibetan. For that, we were blessed to arrive at the bend an hour in advance and without a fine. *How subtle*, W observed astutely. He was hinting that the Tibetan policemen showed grace because I am Tibetan. I assumed he was alluding to our past experience. As the old saying goes, *Policies govern but strategies deal with them.*

In the dark, I stepped into mud and ran to the police checkpoint—a small sentry box by the road—where I had to hand in my papers. A drove on. He bought a new car for this special trip to Tibet. His wife and their four-year-old son were fast asleep. I was the only one spared from altitude sickness. We had left Gormo early in the morning, traveled 900 kilometers, and crossed the Tanggula mountain pass at 5,200 meters above sea level. Under any circumstance, this would be arduous. Much as I hated admitting this, my head was spinning faintly. How guilty I felt—as a Tibetan, I should have gotten over altitude sickness in my homeland long ago.

As we were trying to find accommodation, the flashing red lights of a dozen police cars came toward us out of the blue. Soldiers stood on the roadside. A glimmer of light illumined their shields and guns, as well as their rigid bodies under their coats. I couldn't tell if they were from the People's Armed Police or the People's Liberation Army.[1] When we reached a crossroads, the police—in troops of three to five—were stopping cars and ordering everyone to show their IDS.

You come here, to do what?

The policeman was Tibetan. He spoke in a heavily accented Mandarin and shone his torch to inspect the car.

At that instant, we intuited that we needed a native speaker of Mandarin to speak out for us.

Traveling, W replied.

It did the trick: The policeman waved and let us go. Right in front of us were five men standing by a small lorry, being thoroughly searched by several policemen. Our car drove past them. We could see that they were all young Tibetans. Even though they weren't wearing traditional Tibetan clothes, they—like the policemen—bore the look of Qiang herders. They held their arms up as if to surrender. Since the doom-filled events of March, I was told, Tibetans across the region were compelled to such humiliation while being searched by the police. I had never witnessed this in person and was at once shocked and indignant.

We found a hotel, but the staff were reluctant to bargain. The place stank of tobacco and alcohol. In the middle of the night, we woke to the shrill sirens of police cars. We left Nagchu very early in the morning. Oddly, the awakening streets seemed different from the night before. Police cars and security had disappeared, as if they were never there. All we saw were five or six soldiers with guns and shields, huddled under an umbrella featuring the Olympic mascots.

We spotted a variety of shops: One sold Xi'an snacks, another Hangzhou curtains, yet another with fabric from Guangdong, merchandise from Linxia . . . Turquoise Dumplings was serving breakfast. It had even opened chain outlets all the way from Lhasa to the Changtang. In Lhasa, restaurants had just begun to spring up, and we couldn't help but admire these hardworking people from Sichuan who literally kept their shops open all day long. Ten years ago, during my brief sojourn in Nagchu, we had to travel every day for milk from a herder dressed in a sheepskin robe. Once we followed the herder to the regionally famous Zhapten Monastery, where we offered milk to the Protector deities. Pure and delicious, the milk tasted just like it did in Amdo Labrang, the district of Kanlho, Sangchu, and Nyakchuka in Kardze. Alas, Turquoise Dumplings had since replaced milk with another ingredient. Whether the Protector deities had also modified their diet, I don't know. Banners were apparent in all quarters: The most eye-catching one contained four characters: PUNISH SEVERELY. I'd found out that on April 9, at the crossing next to the adjacent vegetable market, a young boy named Sonam Gyalpo from the Changtang raised his arms and shouted slogans. He was only fifteen when soldiers detained him. To this day, no one knew his whereabouts.

We were given a new registration card for speed limits. By chance we noticed a roadside poster with Drive Safe "propaganda": SLOW DOWN, THERE IS NO HURRY, A PEACEFUL LIFE IS THE KEY TO HAPPINESS;

WHEN THERE IS TRAFFIC, NO NEED TO PANIC, MUTUAL COURTESY WILL
CREATE MORE SPACE FOR EVERYONE, and so on and so forth...Needless
to say, these well-intended messages were written in Chinese—not a word
in Tibetan. So for whom were they meant? Chinese drivers traveling back
and forth? How about Tibetans illiterate in Chinese? In a minority autonomous region where the government claimed to have implemented "regional
administration by the minorities themselves," this was politically incorrect
to say the least. As we passed another poster, I caught a glimpse of its first
sentence: YOU ONLY HAVE ONLY ONE LIFE...a clumsy way to convey the
message that "we" should treasure "our" life. If one risked a car accident,
one might end up losing one's own life and ruining others'. But for us Buddhist Tibetans, life is a circle without an end. Obviously, advertisements
that affirmed life and death in such a didactic manner made no sense to us
Tibetans.

It was drizzling. Black clouds mobbed the sky. A train passed by, then
another...The snowcapped Nyenchen Tanglha mountain range was lost in
the distance. The railway channel was none other than the "Qinghai–Tibet
line": a highway constructed in 1950 between Qinghai and Tibet and a railway built in 2006 between the two regions. The passage ran from Lhasa to
Gormo. All trains from Lhasa to the Chinese mainland departed early in
the morning. But the train service was stopped in March, cutting ties to the
external world. Journalists typically traveled on this train, which now carried only armed soldiers. Little was known outside Tibet since that doom-
filled March.

In use for less than two years, the Qinghai–Tibet railway was now in
military use and control. The authorities must be so proud of this accom-
plishment. Here is a reality censored from the rest of the world: At dawn
on April 25, 675 monks were threatened by armed soldiers, forced to cover
their heads with black cloth, and kidnapped to Lhasa railway station before
being sent to Gormo in a secret run-down train. Yes, a run-down train, not
the modern overnight train for tourists and sightseeing VIPs.

Tibetan monks who left Lhasa in that train and miraculously made their
way back related this story to me in hushed voices. I shut my eyes and vi-
sualized the thousands of Jews packed into trains by the Nazis, who subsequently sent them to concentration camps and crematoriums.

In early April, monks were abducted from their living quarters in the
three main monasteries of Lhasa: Drepung, Sera, and Ganden. In the middle
of the night, armed soldiers, Tibetan policemen, and officers who served as
interpreters or assistants stormed in. More than 675 monks were arrested.

In Drepung Monastery alone, over 700 monks were arrested; in Sera Monastery, over 400, and to this day, we still do not know exactly how many were apprehended from Ganden Monastery. If "only" 675 monks were hauled onto the train, what happened to the rest detained that night?

Probably jailed somewhere in Lhasa . . . alive or dead, no one knows.

I also discovered that on March 10, fourteen monks from Sera Monastery shouted slogans and raised the "snow lion" flag before the Jokhang Temple. Some were sentenced to fourteen-year imprisonment. The youngest, named Lobsang, was fifteen. The eldest, Gelek Bhum, was thirty-two. They came from Kham, not Amdo. I was also told about Lobsang Lhundhup, a monk among them who whispered to himself the night before these tragic events: *We can't go on like this, we really can't, we must stand up!* He hid the Tibetan flag under his clothes the next day, went alone to the Barkhor, and circled the Jokhang Temple. I have two pictures of him, both taken in front of the Potala Palace. He was only twenty-nine and had the whitest teeth I ever saw.

The Chinese authorities removed a hundred teachers from Tibet University and the Traditional Tibetan Medical College and ordered them to teach "legal education" to the 675 monks, now detained in a temporary military prison in Gormo. Classes focused on what was "forbidden," never about the rights entitled to a citizen. These teachers were Tibetans. Imagine how hard it was for them to restrain their emotions and without losing their integrity, faced with monks who suffered such inhumane treatment.

The imprisoned monks were each handed a bilingual Tibetan-Chinese leaflet titled *Rules Governing Student Behavior* that contained only fourteen directives. Line 5 spoke of five "strict forbiddens": For instance, "It is strictly forbidden to break the rules" or "It is strictly forbidden to possess a cutting tool, a cell phone, stones, brick tiles, nails, ropes, medicine, 'counterrevolutionary' books or other prohibited items." Line 12 read, "In the day, one must go to the toilet in groups. At night, one must perform task number 1 or 2 in the dormitory bucket." My jaws dropped. Even the most fundamental physiological needs must be "regulated." Monks were treated as criminals.

After three months, monks from Qinghai were sent home by the regional officials and police. However, their "legal system education" continued under the inspection of the undercover military. The remaining monks had to wait until the end of the Olympics before they could return home. Twenty-four of them who registered their hometown as Rebkong were placed under house arrest in the local middle school of Mepa. Over three hundred from Kham and Amdo Ngaba were put on hold until the end of August before being brought back from different regions as convicts by officials and police.

I visited X under the false identity of a relative. He answered my questions with a painful smile and shared that almost all the monks suffered from heart problems. Jigme Phuntsok, aged twenty-two, from Drepung Monastery, previously from a Buddhist school in Amdo Chentsa, suffered from meningitis but had been misdiagnosed by a nasty military doctor. His health worsened before he eventually died, twenty days later. Another monk, also in his early twenties, couldn't bear the hardship anymore. He hit his head against a wall and was sent to hospital, where he jumped out the window. In the end, he broke his neck and lost his hearing in one ear. I must mention the case of Lobsang and Damdul of Drepung Monastery. Both were formerly from Amdo Ngaba's Kirti Monastery. In fury, they slashed their wrists on March 12. They survived but sustained permanent injuries.

Looking at the Qinghai–Tibet railway, I couldn't picture the monks in the fateful train that abducted them from Lhasa. A fifth-year student at Sera Monastery who affectionately called me *Acha* was arrested the night he had just finished watching the Amdo-Tibetan version of the movie *Braveheart* on his computer.[2] Police and armed soldiers barged into the monastery. Ironically, the cruel reality that he was about to endure mirrored what he saw in the film when Scotland lost its freedom. Calmly the young monk put on his robe and followed the police and soldiers. Little had he imagined that he would relive the fictional scenario ... Another monk, who also called me *Acha*, was a young monk working on his doctorate in the Buddhist school at Drepung Monastery. I last spoke to him on the night of March 10. He told me about the tragedy and how hordes of policemen and soldiers barged into the temple. Detained the longest at the temporary military jail in Gormo, he phoned me while being escorted back to Kham. His voice trembled with panic. He had no idea what to do and where to go. Years ago, he was living a stone's throw from Drepung Monastery, but now he was homeless and without any family. Countless other monks suffered the same fate.

Along the railway, a patrol policeman was present virtually every kilometer. Photos were banned. Yesterday, when we passed by the first police checkpoint after the Tanggula Mountain Pass, one of them on patrol told us frankly that he had been on inspection shifts there every day for over a year now. He mentioned something about the monitors installed along the railway: *Of course we can see very clearly who is responsible for destruction.* Mispronouncing the word *destruction*, which sounded to our ears like "throwing ashes," he came across as a comedian. Despite his military uniform, he was not armed. Instead, he looked like more of a herder and, with his round, tender, delicate face, a rather young herder at that.

Tibetan-style buildings emerged on the roadside: "the new socialist countryside." The place appeared uniform yet industrialized and new. No one knew about the locals being forced off their own lands to give way to these new settlements in the countryside. Ahead of us was Dungkar Village, where I had stayed last summer. It was part of Toelung Dechen district. Tibetans constructed this "new socialist village" from mud and old stones. They gave the village a special name of six characters. The first two characters signified a "very white forehead," which alluded to a loss of fortune or luck. (If one's parents had died prematurely, one would say that one's "forehead has gone white.") The next pair of characters referred to a cow's lungs, intestines, and its other entrails. In the past, only people from modest backgrounds would eat such food, so the term suggested a humble and hard way of life. The last two characters were based on a new term that originated from a popular local custom, a direct reference to a "new building," implying that Tibetan farmers were dissatisfied but couldn't do anything to improve their situation.

I was surprised to find the "international business city" before Dungkar Village done and ready for "consumption." It looked impressive and glittering. Its colorful posters advertised "Great Wall Lubricating Oil," Lanxing cars, Luteshi petroleum, et cetera . . . Most businessmen who resided here were presumably non-Tibetans. When I was here last year, all I saw was a construction site where machines roared and poured concrete. For four weeks, the place was enclosed by Chinese ads and propaganda. One read, ENJOY THE GOVERNMENT'S SPECIAL POLICY: IN THIS SPECIAL AREA, ALL YOU HAVE TO CARE ABOUT IS MAKING MONEY. Another metaphorically encouraged one to plunder: A HINGE IS THE ONLY KEY TO A GOLDEN PLACE; OCCUPY THE PLACE, HOLD THE HINGE. The so-called special area was the homeland of Dungkar villagers. Really, how could villagers forced to leave their homeland enjoy the privileges of the Chinese government's "special policy"?

I interviewed an old couple who were forced out of their home. At first they appeared cautious, even suspicious of me. Little by little, they confided in me about what had happened. Indeed, villagers received a generous compensation from the government to live in these new apartments. However, villagers were paid only 28,000 RMB per acre for their land, which amounted to no more than 45 RMB per square meter. This, as well as the compensation for the construction of these new buildings, would bring the price to less than 60 RMB per square meter. After a year on the stock exchange, the shops of this business city were worth around 6,000 RMB per square meter and rented for 45 RMB per square meter.

Farmers who lost their land only to be offered an apartment in return felt greatly insecure. While they confessed that life in new apartments was more comfortable, they never got used to their modern life. It was nothing compared to the old days when they had their own land. Even though life was harder then, they felt more secure and "down-to-earth." Much as they enjoyed their city-like apartments, they would never become city dwellers. As soon as they heard about the boost in city officials' and workers' wages, they started to fret: The price of market products would escalate too. They couldn't afford beef and butter oil, by now much more expensive than before. Some used money from their land to buy a car in the hope of transforming it into a taxi. Yet they had no clue where to register their taxi business in the city. In the end, they were fined for operating "fake" taxis.

Mothers worried about hunger and poverty. Several families stockpiled mountains of barley harvested from their land. Three years ago, the villagers held four months of discussions with the authorities, hoping to negotiate with the government for the price of 100,000 RMB per acre. A reasonable price, wasn't it? A Tibetan district official who helped villagers with their petition was placed in custody and later fired. Another, a Tibetan woman who worked hard to block the petition, became Lhasa's vice mayor. The last time the villagers tried to meet with the authorities, the president of the Autonomous Region Government yelled at them, "If you come here again, it won't be 28,000 RMB. You won't get even a penny!"

But how would people outside Tibet know any of these stories? All they saw in the media was a five-star flag soaring over the "new socialist village" and a banner on the door of each work unit, wishing success for the Beijing Olympic Games.

Lhasa was now within view. I raced to the last police checkpoint to hand in my speed limit card . . . Was it the tenth, eleventh, or twelfth checkpoint? Before my eyes also appeared the blood and fire of March and the faces of our dear friends arrested in the streets, their homes, or at work. Tears oozed down my cheeks. No one noticed that I was crying: Only I could know how much I missed Lhasa, how much I was hurting for my beloved city . . .

This was my first return to Lhasa for the first time since the outbreak of protests and violence on March 10. It had been five months. Back in my home city, I opened my heart to its mountains and breathed the air that gave Lhasa its distinct odor. Once again, I could hear the familiar accent of Lhasa and feel its pulse. Given that we'd been away from Lhasa since the previous September, I was now a mere spectator who had to rely on memories and the accounts of other reliable witnesses during this time. How I wished I'd stayed here with my own people. I despaired at my efforts, ashamed of my inadequacy and absence.

Going westward in the direction of the memorial of the Qinghai–Sichuan–Tibet Highway, we took the only route available to us. I looked out: Both sides of the road were packed with at least five large army troops whose barracks took up most of the space. It was hard to tell how many soldiers were stationed there. Each main entrance was guarded by at least four armed soldiers. Since 1959, the hub of Lhasa had been a military center, as were other Tibetan cities. From Norbulingka Road to the Potala Square, we arrived at the crossroads of Chakpori Hill, face to face with armed soldiers staring back at us. They were the first soldiers we met in Lhasa. This was a prelude, the tip of the iceberg: our first brush against the killing machine.

I took a picture of the Chinese flag flying above the Potala Palace, another of the Olympic banner at the foot of the holy site. Ten characters decorated with flowers were inscribed on it: MINORITIES UNITE AS ONE MIND TO GREET THE OLYMPICS. Several women of my mother's generation were prostrating. But they weren't prostrating to the red flag or the Olympic banner: They were prostrating to the Potala Palace, or, to be precise, the Dalai Lama, who once resided there. Vacant since 1959, enveloped in dust, the site remained the seat of His Holiness, forever engraved in our Tibetan memory and collective consciousness.

We proceeded east and stopped at Serkhang Hotel to help A's family settle in. There we could bargain for 120 RMB per night. This would have been impossible a year before, but tourism had dwindled so drastically that it would take more than a month before business recovered, by which it would soon be winter, the offseason. As it turned out, now was the perfect time for A to visit Lhasa with his wife and son. A year ago, he would have "seen" little of Lhasa beyond non-Tibetan tourists like himself. What was the point of being part of a mass of tourists in search of an imaginary Shangri-la?

In any case, there was no way for the authorities to set a new record for tourism in Tibet that year. Just a few days before March 14, during the annual "Two Sessions" meeting of the Chinese Parliament in Beijing, the official Jampa Phuntsok announced, "Train transportation brings significant tourism to Tibet: Last year the number of tourists reached a peak of 4 million.

Next to Tibet's 1.2 million square area, however, this is nothing . . . Even with a few more million tourists, Tibet would hardly be affected."

Had there been *a few more million tourists* visiting Tibet, wouldn't the Potala Palace be inundated with streams of tourists unable to move or breathe? According to 2007 media statistics, more than 1.6 million tourists visited the Potala Palace. But the figures seemed dubious: The Potala Palace was typically the first destination for the annual 4 million tourists in Tibet. Rarely would one visit Tibet without touring the Potala. During the peak season, the locals made profits by purchasing cheap tickets, then selling them at an exorbitant price. A "mere" 1.6 million tourists visiting the Potala would translate into more than 4,400 visitors each day, far exceeding the related department figures of 2,300 visitors per day. Some years ago, the management department in charge of the Potala made it clear that it wasn't feasible for the historical architecture to handle more than 800 visitors per day. Parts of the building had since collapsed.

Serkhang Hotel was located east of the bustling market. Farther off was the old Tibetan town that was at the center of the unrest in March. When I brought up the subject, the Tibetan waitress raised her hand and pointed at a black building now veiled by a huge plastic cover. Once a restaurant, it was now the "evidence" of the "burning and looting" of March 14, she said. Presumably, the authorities wanted to preserve the building and turn it into yet another symbolic site for "patriotic education." Perhaps it wasn't too bad an idea to preserve the place as "a site of memory for minorities": It could serve as a physical reminder to us Tibetans of the March 14 bloodshed. Wouldn't this also fulfill its "pedagogical" mission?

To the west of Serkhang Hotel was a compound where luxuriant gardens existed before the 1959 uprising. Now no more than a cluster of dilapidated houses, it was once the living quarters of the Dalai Lama's family. Today it was enclosed by Tibetan boutiques, American ice cream shops, and a Dicos fast-food restaurant. Five women working at a nearby boutique were burned to death on March 14. Three women who set the shop ablaze were eventually arrested. Allegedly they had been working there for some time and wanted to take revenge when the shopkeeper embezzled part of their wages. They set fire to the shop, but had no intention of harming anyone. I was told those five women were burned upstairs while the shopkeeper fled for his own life, locking the door behind him. In one blaze, eight—not five—young lives were stolen. The shopkeeper Shi acted remorseful in front of the cameras and ended up cashing in all profits: The government granted him a rebate of 1 million RMB in a loan. He set up a new shop elsewhere and resumed business in no time. But his business never recovered: Tibetans secretly agreed to boycott the new but jinxed shop.

My home was located behind the Potala Palace in a district called New Shol Village. After almost a year, here I was, back at last . . . The moment I saw my beautiful mother, I had the feeling that things would turn out fine. Despite her anxiety, Mother didn't seem to have aged much. I hugged her and heaved a sigh of relief. Never would I have thought that we'd part again, in less than a week, as she took my hand and said, "Today's Lhasa is no longer last year's Lhasa. You too aren't who you were last year." I was speechless. My mother never lied.

September 2008, Beijing

NOTES

1. The People's Armed Police (PAP) is as one of the three main branches of the Chinese armed forces, responsible for internal and maritime securities and for supporting the People's Liberation Army (PLA) during wartime.

2. *Acha* is Tibetan for "older sister."

18

The Killing Trip

I bumped into my young cousin Gyatso in a bar near my workplace. After a light chat, he invited me on the spur of the moment on a trip to Terdrom Hot Spring the next day. The place, he said, would appeal to my taste. At once I began to romanticize about a luxurious relaxation at a steamy mountain spring glittering under the peaceful moon, and without any hesitation I agreed.

Terdrom Hot Spring is located in Meldro Gungkar County to the east of Lhasa. To be accurate, it lies in a meandering valley around 150 kilometers outside Lhasa. Just a stone's throw from the county, however, the path proves to be either muddy or rocky as it turns left, not to mention that parts of it are often flooded—gullied in summer and frozen in winter—so it isn't unheard of for one to walk at least five or six hours before reaching this promising scenic spot.

Despite the obstacles, people and cars flock to this path all year long in hope of visiting the well-known historical sites deep in those mountains. The main highlight is Drigung Til Monastery, an ancestral monastery of the Drigung Kagyu—one of the four Tibetan Buddhist schools—and the largest sky-burial site in Tibet. Tibetans hold this particular sky-burial site in high esteem, as they believe the souls of those brought here after death will attain enlightenment sooner. Metaphorically, the Drigung Kagyu sky-burial site is their "handy ladder" between two realms or worlds.

It is no coincidence, then, that Terdrom Hot Spring lies within the vicinity. Like a typical hot spring, it boasts several health benefits and healing powers, particularly in spring and autumn. More crucially, Terdrom Hot Spring is noted for its religious significance. Over twelve centuries ago, Padmasambhava, the founder of Vajrayana Buddhism—known as Guru Rin-

poche to Tibetans—took refuge in Terdrom, where he lived in retreat for years. He threw his *dorje* at a cliff,[1] splitting the cliff into two before snow atop the mountain melted and slid toward the farmlands. The earth shook violently. Bubbles of steam burst from the surface. Imagine the soothing effects of this hot spring after soaking in it, in addition to its miraculous healing power.

This said, not everyone back then was entitled to bathe in this hot spring. Rocks were amassed to separate the area into two. Traditionally, only high lamas such as the most noble lamas from Drigung Til could soak in the upper spring; the lower spring was for the secular aristocrats. Needless to say, there was no place for the lowly commoners. It's unclear how it became accessible to any Tom, Dick, and Harry—could it have happened after the "revolutionary liberation of a million serfs"? Perhaps, and why not? But what about the water quality when the public has become so diverse? Might it be "polluted," its healing power weakened? Furthermore, why should the upper spring be reserved exclusively for men, the lower spring for women? Water runs unquestionably from high to low; is it thus implied that men might be "cleaner," "purer," or "loftier" than women? Some speak of a Tibetan belief that water cleanses itself once it flows beyond a step, but how is this possible? Regardless, such bathing "protocol" seems rather strange, to say the least. Unless one is out there alone in the spring, it must have felt awkward with others around staring.

I've visited Terdrom Hot Spring twice, first in the early summer of 1995, when I had to take a public van, which moved at such an excruciatingly slow pace that I could keep writing. In those days, both the upper and lower springs were "open air"—in other words, "naked in broad daylight." No big deal for anyone to peek at another's nudity. Tiny creepy snakes slithered on rocks nearby. I'd have been frightened to death had I not been assured that they were benign.

My second visit took place two springs ago. It was snowing. Two naked foreign women burst out of nowhere amid the foggy steam just as I was about to take the plunge into the spring. Snowflakes fell onto their bodies before melting at first touch while they chuckled and giggled nonstop. How eventful.

On both occasions, I stayed with an *ani* in a hut.[2] Let me introduce the nunnery nearby. Also of the Drigung Kagyu lineage, it teaches from the

Nyingma School as well. Over the mountain slope facing the hot spring are scattered red huts owned by nuns much prettier than others elsewhere. It must have something to do with the nourishing hot spring. I lodged in a traditional Tibetan hut within walking distance from the spring. It was rather convenient for me to take a bath, but a nightmare for sleep—literally. At nightfall, dogs barked ceaselessly. In Terdrom, there were many dogs which wouldn't bite but would irritate and follow you everywhere. More than that, there were lots of night visitors who chatted late into the night and made a riot of footsteps. . . .

Well, I also bathed in the hot spring late at night. Of course I minded the water running down from the upper "men's" spring, but in the wee hours I couldn't resist soaking and indulging myself in the warm spring—all on my own. A clear spring sparkled under the moon. I could even count its pebbles. Gazing at the silvery stars and skies in a fog of steam, amid the synchronized sounds of water and faint barking of dogs, I couldn't help but sigh in contentment after calming my body and mind in sheer joy.

Of all wonders of nature I've known or visited, Terdrom Hot Spring is my favorite.

The next day was Saturday. We had agreed to leave at ten. But I waited until midday and still no one showed up. Quietly, I mocked how we Tibetans were born with no concept of time and thought of W, who often described us as a people lacking "numerized" management. At first I felt inclined to defend my kin, but the truth eventually spoke for itself.

At last, my cousin Gyatso appeared in a Volkswagen with four other Tibetan lads, three of whom were dressed in handsome *pagtsag*, a traditional Tibetan garment, coupled with a fur-lined lambskin jacket and a woolen shirt of satin stand-up collar and slant flaps, inlaid with a brocade. *Pagtsag* used to be a winter clothing for the elderly, and it had been in vogue among young Tibetans in Lhasa these recent years. They varied in colors and quality and were rather expensive; an excellent *pagtsag*, for instance, cost over a thousand yuan.

Not only were these young men dressed identically; they also, to my surprise, had an almost identical upbringing. Born in the 1970s, they studied at Tibetan high schools in China and returned to work in Lhasa upon college or technical institute graduation. Nowadays they and men like them have either resigned from public service to be their own bosses or have kept their jobs while making money on the side. Coming from wealthy cadre families, they strive to be enterprising and successful "model examples." Born as "emancipated serfs," their parents love the Communist Party. In return, the Party grants them "special treatment," which is why their children grow up with a superiority complex. They have a highly efficient network of contacts and stand out from typical Tibetan youths in Lhasa.

Tsewang, for instance, used to work as bank cashier. His relatives include bureau director X and government official Y. In addition, he was once the classmate of the son of the most powerful Tibetan, Secretary Ragdi. Next, we have Dhargyal with his glasses, the son of some high-ranking official who joined them in opening inns, bars, and other business ventures. They now run a travel agency and have named it Terdrom. It beats me why they would set their eyes on Terdrom.

Despite its hot spring fame, Terdrom is until today deprived of roads, electricity, and phone lines. The Meldro Gungkar County government was informed of its market value, the lucrative publicity due to its "brand name," and its ideal geomantic placing, yet failed to make much progress in this remote area. This is the case for most of Tibet's basic development: It could never expand beyond the county if not spurred on by the opportunistic projects of people like Tsewang. As it turned out, Tsewang and others had invested 800,000 to 900,000 yuan on a large patch of land encircling the hot spring in view of a hotel, on phone lines, highway construction, and a mini–power station. Considering the land size and their forty-year lease, their expenses were practically peanuts. Moreover, all procedures would be authorized by the state, so no doubt they had all the back doors open to them. To all Tibetan officials, Secretary Ragdi is a big-shot household name: What restrictions could his son possibly face in Tibet?

The trip was none other than Tsewang the deputy boss's idea: He planned to show my cousin Gyatso around to convince him to become their management consultant. For years, Gyatso had been working in a hotel in Lhasa, once an assistant to the director before his promotion as a manager of some entertainment department. Goodness knows what else he had been up to since then. In any case, he excelled at Chinese and English, compared to his rusty Tibetan.

The other two young men were Pasang and Sherab. Pasang was one of these "elites" working in a Tibet Autonomous Region bureau. Sherab, on the other hand, had a nonchalant air, different attire, and looked rather ordinary. He spoke using street slang, throwing in words such as *kunchok* or *ye-she*.[3] He appeared to be more knowledgeable about monasteries and lamas than his friends; I even mistook him for a religious young man until Gyatso mentioned that he worked in the Security Department as a stationmaster at a post on the border.

I naively thought Gyatso had invited me along for a bath in the hot spring. After all, among my cousins in Lhasa, he and I got along rather well. I've always found him boyish despite his towering height. Little had I expected that he was in fact hoping I could write something about Terdrom Hot Spring—no, his Terdrom Travel Agency. Nowhere in this world could he imagine that "the piece" I wrote would turn out to be this "political fiction."

"*Acha*," he said coaxingly. "If you really want to write about Tibet, write about us, the young generation. We're the true masters of its future."

I paid him no heed at first, but after our short trip, I felt deeply hurt and upset.

It started to feel like a joke when I was told that we would hang around the city before leaving for Terdrom. As if to defer to the Tibetan daily ritual of drinking sweet tea, they needed a few drinks. So we drove to a teahouse named Revolution at an old street in the Barkhor.

The four of us squeezed like sardines into the back seats. Since Gyatso and I were skinny, we occupied less than a single seat for a fat person. But the policeman disagreed: Seeing us dig our way out of such a small car, he sternly gestured to us.

"Dumbass," muttered Dhargyal before stumbling forth to greet them.

The rest of the group pretended as if nothing had happened. Wrapped in a large coat, the policeman looked like a sore iron tower. No one could tell if he was Tibetan or Han Chinese. He bowed politely before speaking fast to Dhargyal. Once the policeman was done with his monologue, Dhargyal too made a quick bow before the others rushed over to encircle them. I started to have cold feet. Gyatso assured me that it was all right and that they would "take the matter into their own hands." Sure enough, they returned with smiling faces and even made way for the policeman to drive off "proudly."

"No problem, let's go in for tea. Dhargyal will take care of everything," Tsewang spoke loudly as he made his way toward Revolution.

Revolution enjoys an established reputation among the teahouses in Lhasa. In truth, it isn't all that "established," since one can guess from its name when it first came in existence. Compared to the famous Lugtsang [Sheep Pen] or Gamchung [Small Box], it isn't historic but is immensely popular among the locals. All old teahouses look alike: dark, suffocating, filthy with their rickety long tables and benches, flies in summer and beggars in winter. Nevertheless, they are the centers where people gather for gossip and news. In the heat of true and false rumors and surreal oddities, a cup of tea at twenty or thirty cents tastes exquisite. Pronounced in a distinct Tibetan accent, even the Chinese word "Revolution" sounds exotic and magnetic. In fact, Revolution enjoys such popularity that a second branch has opened in Lhasa.

Everyone in Lhasa is addicted to this English black tea, sugared and with milk (even though the "milk" they use nowadays is just milk powder). Women were conventionally forbidden in teahouses, where they would be perceived as "loose." Today, on account of the change of winds and customs, what a Tibetan male comrade can do, a Tibetan woman cadre is just as capable of, never mind going to Revolution. Teahouses open for business early in the day and serve mostly elders who are on their way to do their circumambulations. At other times, they are frequented by people from all walks of life. Most Tibetans spend as much time in teahouses as at their work units.

Not far from our table was a group of young men and women talking and laughing boisterously. They spoke in Chinese, perfecting each word as best as they could, and from time to time mixed them with some Tibetan. With disdain, Pasang or Sherab pointed them out as students from the nearby Tibet University. We each ordered a three-pound flask of sweet tea and a bowl of beef rib soup noodles. As thick as chopsticks, those Tibetan noodles were handmade by Tibetans, not by the Chinese or Muslims. Back to join us, Dhargyal threw his keys on the table and yelled, "How dare he accuse me of violating highway code A, B, C. He had nothing to say once I had a word with his boss."

It was half past one in the afternoon. The sun shone high. At last we were ready for Terdrom.

As we approached Lhasa Bridge, Pasang in the front seat flashed out a hand grenade firecracker.

"Let's blow it up," he suggested excitedly.

Tsewang stopped him. "Can't you see the soldiers guarding the bridge? They will arrest us if we do it right now. Let's play with it after passing the bridge."

Once past the bridge, the grenade firecracker exploded along our way: dumping sites piled with plastic bags, oil depots, villages, small shops, hidden military camps, farms, ruins atop hills, freshly painted monasteries, and rows of brick buildings in the county. None of these was a target for the boys, who instead aimed at voyagers like us: farmers on horse-drawn carts or tractors, bus passengers who had stopped to rest, teams of contract migrant workers, nomadic monks in red robes, sneezing children, and so on. Whenever they ran into any worker who looked Sichuanese or Han Chinese, Sherab would yell, "Let's blow them up!" All of them were so frightened by the exploding firecrackers that they froze or screamed before taking to their heels. Pigs, dogs, cows, goats, and dogs were not spared, either.

Laughter louder than the exploded firecrackers thundered throughout our journey. Every time Pasang pulled the string to throw a firecracker out of the window, the rest of them would stretch their necks out, overjoyed. Although I knew that these grenades were fake and the boys were just playing pranks, I felt awkward and anxious, for fear of firecrackers exploding in our car by mistake.

As I've mentioned, traveling from the county to Terdrom wasn't an easy task. Naturally, our Volkswagen couldn't make it through, but the boys had made the arrangements in advance. As soon as we reached Meldro Gungkar County, we switched to a Toyota suv owned by the local tax bureau. Relieved that they had run out of explosive grenade firecrackers, I couldn't believe my eyes when the exultant Dhargyal pulled out a small-bore rifle from the trunk.

"What for?" I asked.

"To hunt," he responded bluntly. He must have found my question redundant. Someone chipped in about "killing some cackling chicken."

My heart sank.

The trip of gunpowder and slaughter had begun. I couldn't have dreamed that these mild-looking young Tibetans who spoke in chic Tibetan and Chinese would turn out to be barbarians. Little could I have imagined that they were my own cousin Gyatso and his friends.

Appalled and troubled by their savage behavior, I grew more disgusted by the minute. As we passed a mountain slope sprawling with shrubs, the first kill finally appeared. It was a rabbit, a silly rabbit that exposed itself right in the open as if to invite its predators. Dhargyal braked and leaped out with his rifle. Unlike in a movie, where the hunter would creep up cautiously, all he did was walk up with his rifle raised. The rabbit was shot in its hind leg.

"Stop!" I cried.

Too late. My weak yells were drowned in their ecstasy.

I couldn't stomach the sight. Relentless, Dhargyal pursued the rabbit with his rifle. Where could the poor creature go? Limping with an injured leg, it was killed on the spot in the next few shots.

I couldn't see the rabbit lying in pain on the grass, but could imagine the killer's cold-blooded gaze behind his glasses. Not a second of doubt. Step by step, in pure violence. Euphoric, the others dashed out of the car to pick up the rabbit. I was flabbergasted. That was a life: free in its own world before an abrupt bloody death.

A Buddhist by faith, I was so pained and frustrated with what I saw. I was taught to accept love for all beings. By "beings," I refer not just to us mankind but also creatures flying in the sky, crawling aground, swimming in the water. . . . Creatures such as the rabbit could have been related to me in our previous lives, or, who knows, my kin. In which case, would I have run into the rabbit were we not linked by fate or karma? But what did I do except let it die such a tragic death right before my eyes? Why didn't I do something? I couldn't believe that all I did was to utter a futile *Stop*. What kind of Buddhist was I, if not an accomplice?

Throughout the rest of our ride, I was livid. I said nothing until we were stopped by two nuns carrying food and beef. Dhargyal—again it was Dhargyal—alighted. With a smile, he helped to load their belongings into our car so they could walk to the hot spring without burden. Granted his small act of kindness, I decided to forgive him and the boys, and began conversing with them. I tried not to think about the bloody rabbit that had been thrown into the trunk.

We finally reached our destination. I could feel none of the joy I experienced from my earlier visits. It was already seven in the evening. The sun had yet to set. Surveying from the mountain, I saw the vanishing path and the piercing shine of corrugated iron sheet roofs. Tsewang pointed at them and said, "That's our hotel." He was glowing with pride.

I lamented, "Why iron sheet roofs? How incongruous with the rest of this wilderness."

Tsewang insisted, "It's practical to build hotels with such roofs. Those old Tibetan roofs leak. There's so much rainfall in summer here."

"Maybe," I casually replied. "But really, the color is so ugly."

As before, the nuns' huts were scattered like rubies over the slope, as if to comfort our eyes, which hurt from the piercing reflection of those iron sheet roofs. Down the slope we saw the steamy hot spring surrounded by cliffs now swathed in prayer flags and rows of small inns. The hot spring was no longer in the "open air." Half of it was blocked by a lofty wooden frame to discourage Peeping Toms.

"How unique," I mumbled. A positive change for once.

There were two kinds of hotels in Terdrom: the new concrete houses built by Tsewang and others, and those old-style Tibetan huts run by the nunnery. What an irony: While those clean, new houses were empty and deserted, the cluttered Tibetan huts, like some unearthed archaeological treasures, were housed with foreigners in *pagtsag*. The latter must have been more affordable, I reckoned. Besides, tourists were attracted to "authenticity," whatever that meant.

In exasperation, green with envy, Tsewang complained, "These nuns are dumb heads. We've negotiated with them several times and asked them to raise their prices. Of course people would rather stay with them. Our rooms cost sixty yuan each, theirs ten! But really, they're so dumb! All their rent added up isn't enough to pay for two of our rooms. Come high season, I'm sure our rooms will be fully booked. They might as well just sell their houses to us and not bother themselves with making business."

"So why didn't you buy them?" I provoked him.

"Because they're afraid of us bullying them into it," explained Tsewang. "In the past all this land belonged to the nunnery. With the hot spring open to the public, the county was the first to build a guesthouse here. They agreed to share the money with the nunnery. Not a cent, in the end. Ever since, the nuns have been tough. They'd rather earn little than to be cheated by empty promises."

"Well, we do want to take advantage of them, don't we?" Dhargyal chuckled. "How can they dream of making any decent business in such a place? Who cares if they don't give in to us now? In no time, we 'the city' will sweep it all away."

We were savoring tea in a nun's hut as we spoke. Since there were no clients at Tsewang's new hotel, the innkeeper declared a vacation and went home. We had no choice but to spend a night in a hut owned by the nuns. I saw the boys chatting and joking with the nuns, and mistakenly thought they were being kind. Abashed, three young nuns covered their mouths with their hands as they laughed, and kept serving us hot butter tea. They even cooked a bowl of instant noodles for each of us. How on earth would they ever suspect them of any evil intention when the boys spoke only in Chinese? The nuns understood nothing they said.

We stewed beef bought in the county and served it with chili sauce and buns. How delicious. The moon rose. Time for a bath in the hot spring.

Two candles glowed softly by the misty spring. A warmth I had long yearned for soon dispersed the cold spell around me. Under the moonlight, the spring water felt so much more exhilarating and uplifting. I couldn't swim but moved around by stepping clumsily on a few coarse yet slippery rocks. The water was clean and hot, emanating a gentle force that, in Buddhist belief, embraces every single life and tolerates all in the three realms of existence.

Nuns bathing in the spring began to sing in subdued but mesmerizing voices. Their dharma chants praised Guru Rinpoche and sounded much like mountain folk songs or love ballads. An old lady came along too. Like most women in the grazing land, she wrapped herself in thick lambskin, revealing her slim figure once she took off her clothes. Her silhouette swayed and radiated with the beauty of youth. Before taking leave, they kindly instructed me not to linger too long in the spring for fear of panic attack.

Here I was, on my own once more, indulging in the warmth of this blessed water. I could not help but think of my lover, a non-Tibetan far away in his hometown. How I wished he could join me here. How I wished for a perfect life.

I spent the night by myself in a hut with six beds but no door latch. Every bed was caked in dust and mud off the ceiling or walls. I had brought along my sleeping bag. As a seasoned traveler, I had learned to make myself at home wherever I went.

I woke up first thing in the morning and enjoyed myself in the hot spring when no one was around yet. Then I took my camera up the mountain behind the monastery. Suddenly I caught sight of Dhargyal darting past the monastic tower with a rifle. How could he have the heart to kill in a sacred place? Joy and peace vanished from me at once. Monasteries in Tibet are meant to be a paradise for animals. I even knew a far-flung monastery where the fish leaped onto a lama's hand to munch on tsampa, Tibetan roasted barley flour. Terdrom, on the contrary, was now reduced to a Disneyland for hunters.

Farther up the nuns' red huts behind the monastery lie caves for hermits. Legend has it that the incarnation of Guru Rinpoche's *dakini* Yeshe Tsogyal lives there:[4] a seventy-year-old *khandroma*.[5] Unfortunately, she was in retreat whenever I visited. I guess I wasn't destined to cross paths with her. In my memory, I was lying on my own on the same mountain slope five years ago, gazing at white rocks carved with the characters OM MANI PADME HUM, watching nuns dressed in red carry water home. Time blurred in these seemingly identical surroundings. In Tibet, time behaves differently than elsewhere. It bends like a wire bent into a circle. It flows like sour milk spilled over the floor. All feels almost timeless and stilled.

On my way back to the nunnery, I bumped into Gyatso and Tsewang. To me, the monastery was a home where I could speak from my heart. I thought of the mandala of Guru Rinpoche, his twenty-five godly disciples, and his eight different manifestations. Sungma. Yidam. Khandroma. My protectors. I couldn't resist speaking my mind.

"Tsewang, since you're doing business in a holy place, you must respect its sacred ground in order to receive blessings and protection." I was hoping they could show mercy and stop their killing.

Tsewang stared at me. "Well, I should worship this Guru Rinpoche, then!" He continued, "I've never visited monasteries before. All thanks to this Terdrom, I must now keep visiting monasteries." It goes without saying that he visited the monastery for reasons different from mine.

Like many other monasteries in Tibet, this nunnery is tiny and austere. Monasteries are a spiritual refuge for local common folks, who support them in return. In theory, monasteries practice the tradition of self-sufficiency, but in reality they barely get by on their own. Life in nunneries is even harder. One can't imagine how important this hot spring is to these nuns and their survival. There is no reason they shouldn't try to make a living by selling en-

trance tickets to hot spring visitors. Alas, they probably can't even save their modest red huts from inevitable destruction.

We left Terdrom at noon. Pasang carried the rifle lackadaisically while the rest paced around the car, for fear of letting go of any prey. On purpose, I began to spin a yarn about karma. I spoke of my uncle who suffered from cancer. He killed countless musk deer, wild deer, and foxes when young and starving. A stranger, also a Rinpoche, told him the illness was his karma for the lives he took, and only by releasing captive animals could he enjoy a longer life.[6] So his family bought fish every day to release them in the river. My uncle died two years later.

   Tibetans believe in these stories as some kind of forewarning. To be religious and pious, one needs to be rigorous and disciplined in life. To loosely quote from one of the Dalai Lama's teachings, "Once a person puts one's heart into the precepts, self-restraint and abstinence will take place on their own, even in moments of negative thoughts." Because of the role of religion in a true Tibetan life, we must commit ourselves to the Buddhist doctrine on several levels; above all, one must never take a life. From any perspective of spiritual redemption, killing imbues the worst karma. *You reap what you sow:* This is an interrelated chain of karma. Buddhism is based on the teachings of respect and empathy, including self-respect and self-empathy, the only way to the perfection of life.

Thou shalt not kill: Not only does one realize the fragility and value of human life, one learns to view other frail forms of life as equally important. Disrespect for any nonhuman life translates into a disrespectful being on all accounts. What an excellent commandment. It teaches us to practice tolerance, respect, humility, and gratitude, without which we are devoid of self-control, only to be filled with arrogance, aggression, disdain, destruction, and hatred. A writer whose name I can't recall off the top of my head has this to say: "The destruction of life is a fascist game."

I had no intention of portraying myself as the flattering image of a moralist or holy being. I evoked karma to alert myself. I was conscious of my vulnerability, and how as a passive bystander I had witnessed the killing of a poor rabbit. I had no desire to be their spectator again. Whatever I saw was a burden enough.

My words fell on deaf ears. These young men were governed by nothing more than their own cravings and the illusion of happiness. To them, since killing could meet one's desire and bring joy, however short-lived, there was no reason not to kill. They were too eager to kill. One rabbit wasn't enough. In no time, they found their new victims: a rabbit idle in the grass and a wild chicken. Nor did they spare a pigeon in a barley-threshing ground: It fell right to its death in the pull of a trigger. I hadn't even finished my story about karma. What a fool I was to think that it would produce any effect on these sinicized, Westernized, modernized young Tibetans.

A few slender black birds wandered gracefully around the weeds.

"Black-necked cranes!" exclaimed Dhargyal. Again the thirst to hunt and kill.

"No, not this one!" I shouted so vehemently that I could even hear my voice turning hoarse.

Dhargyal stopped short. "Of course." He pretended and said, "No one wants to go to jail for having killed these poor little creatures." And he drove on.

I almost asked, "Did you say that you didn't want to kill only because you're afraid of *going to jail*?"

Cries of the crane broke through the space. But what did I mean by *not this one*? Did I suggest that others could be killed instead? How absurd.

Without warning, the tire went flat. A sandstorm was gathering. The skies and the road were instantly enveloped in dust. The boys started to panic. I couldn't help but rejoice in their misfortune.

"See," I declared. "That's your karma."

Cousin Gyatso nudged at me, hinting that I should keep my mouth shut. Even though his gunshots had missed, he was sticking up for those sinners.

After a torturous hours-long wait, we were back on the road. Soon we arrived at Meldro Gungkar. Switching back to the Volkswagen, the boys started to throw their "stags" out of the trunk and onto the ground. Two rabbits, a pigeon, and a chicken, each with bullet holes and soaked in blood, creatures once so beautiful out there in the world, but now stiff and still on this cold ground. *No big deal*—I could imagine my cousin teasing me. *But is this* not *a "big deal"*? I asked myself. *Aren't these lives? Aren't we our own murderers who butcher our own empathy and hearts in turn?*

No longer could I bear their cruelty. Swarmed by anger, I'd hardly relaxed a moment. Nothing of this trip to Terdrom Hot Spring had turned out as I'd expected. I felt even angrier with myself: Why didn't I stop them from taking lives? Was I afraid of their violence? Or because I didn't know how to stop them from their own violence? How dare they impose their cruelty on a third party by compelling me to witness and participate in their killing game?

That wasn't the end of it. Once began, the game accelerated. Their faces burned aglow with violence and the thirst for violence. Along the way from Meldro Gungkar to Lhasa, winter pastures littered with puddles contrasted with the distant meandering brooks. A paddling of ducks floated on water. Just a day ago, the boys were mocking how "emotional" these creatures were, always in pairs; when one was shot, the other would swirl around its dead partner passionately before taking its last breath. The boys howled and leaped out of their car and aimed at a yellow duck before pulling the trigger.

Enough.

Infuriated, I slammed the car door, grabbed my backpack from the trunk, and walked away. The sandstorm threatened again. Wind and sand. In this wind and sand, dusk appeared to be shrouded in gunpower smoke from all directions, inscrutable and impenetrable. My face was soaked with tears. Since when was I part of such company? How on earth could I associate with these people? What compassion did these self-confessed "masters of the future Tibet" show for their own homeland? Would they not stop unless their country was reduced to a slaughterhouse and dust?

At last, they called it a day. Without a word, they sulked and walked back to the car. Cousin Gyatso caught up with me.

"All right, no more hunting!" he said. "Let's get back to the car together. Let's return to Lhasa." He looked guilty and embarrassed. I relented. Let's return to Lhasa with our four dead rabbits, pigeon, and chicken to cook and serve with wine and butter. Prayers drowned by deafening party music and dance, Lhasa was no longer the paradise, the sacred and pure land of the immortals. To whom could it entrust its destiny? Where would its future go?

Let's return to Lhasa.

January 13, 2001—Lhasa

NOTES

1. A *dorje* is a thunderbolt used in rituals. [author's note]

2. *Ani* is Tibetan for "nun."

3. *Kunchok* is Tibetan for "I swear by the Three Jewels." *Yeshe* is Tibetan for "I swear before Shakyamuni or the Dalai Lama." [author's note]

4. *Dakini* is Sanskrit for "Tibetan angel or consort."

5. *Khandroma* is Tibetan for *dakini.*

6. The Tibetan term for releasing captive animals—"animal release" or "life liberation"—is *tsethar.*

19

Few Years Later

Few years later
you're at the original site
I'm at its opposite end
on a plane
in a car
also arriving at the original site

Few years later
you've aged
I've aged
We seem to age at the same time
still young
and with a temper

Few years later
I'm covered with dust
and disfigured
Yet I insist on looking elegant
using postiche bones
as jewelry
wearing them on my chest
as if with nonchalance

Few years later
your face
looks so clean
scholarly
like tears from inside
an extra sheen
you can't wipe dry

Few years later
we sit together at last
first a little distant
then slightly closer
Voices around us
are grotesque and gaudy
I want to speak but hesitate
You want to speak but hesitate
What else could we say

October 1990, Chengdu

20

Masks and Tea

1

Some prefer a tiger, its golden skin
Some prefer an elephant, its circumambulation
I prefer a snow leopard
its blue-green mane
I dream of it every night

2

Am I the only one who sees ruins
the wreckage
unable to recover from shock
while you turn a blind eye, safe and sound
or pretend all's fine

3

Shops cluster around Jebumgang Police Station
Masked plastic mannequins dressed in the old days
men and women, in their prime years
half-smiling
the mystery of a smile

4

Strive for the better
Free yourself of this dark underground
Endless maggots wriggle
I can't even kill one
Is the intent to kill a violation

5

Seen/unseen, seen/unseen
a red flag in green woods
I can't call out the trees by their names
A gust shatters them
Five stars glitter eerily on the flag

6

This pandemic, an invisible evil
waiting for the opportunity to attack, attack
How can a leaky mask over a face
block out infected spurt
We must find the real talisman

7

On this full moon night
please give me a cup of Four Noble Truths
Just a sip—I want to give
such precious tea to my kin
for a reunion in this liberated world

    September 21–October 3, 2020—Shanghai

21

An Eye from History and Reality

Woeser and Her Story of Tibet

Originally conducted in Chinese, this interview appeared in an early form in *Cerise Press* (vol. 3, no. 9) in the spring of 2012. Below is an expanded version that includes questions from additional interviews conducted via Skype and email in the winter months of 2018 and 2022–23.

DECHEN PEMBA AND FIONA SZE-LORRAIN: *You studied literature and first worked as a journalist before becoming an editor for a literary journal in Lhasa. When did you discover a love for poetry as well as your own voice as a poet?*

TSERING WOESER: I have loved stories since I was a child. My earliest memory is of telling the story of the time before I left Lhasa, to a bunch of children in Tawo County, Sichuan. I was only four or five. When evoking Lhasa I would often invent some intrigue to attract friends. My storytelling made me yearn for Lhasa.

Alas, I can now no longer locate the first poem I wrote. I remembered writing it in Tawo County while in my first year of middle school. The news had just broadcast the death of a famous Chinese poet. I felt a little sad, so I wrote a few lines that resembled the arrangement of a poem. To me, it felt like a poem.

However, among the poems I now archive, the earliest is one I wrote in 1984 as a first-year student at the faculty of Chinese language at the Southwest University for Nationalities. Among my classmates were students from more than ten "minority" groups and those of the Han Chinese majority. This poem is titled "Seal—for Certain Prejudices." I vaguely remember arguing with a few Han Chinese classmates and writing this poem on the spot, then copying it painstakingly on the blackboard. They were shocked.

Revisiting this tender poem now, I'm surprised that I had already found a national consciousness at eighteen. It's also clear to me now that I've always turned to poetry to express my voice.

SEAL

FOR CERTAIN PREJUDICES

Never again let
disdain's muddy water
flow from your young eyes
The seal exudes
the scent of butter tsampa
engraved on my heart
I do not despair
I even refuse your cold
glance

Perhaps
a natural sense of superiority
bloats your life
But I won't
offer a complying smile
Sun
shines on you, shines on me
On a blue planet
we are equal![1]

In truth, during my college years I'd started writing poetry seriously and organized a poetry club with classmates from all different majors and ethnic groups who shared my passion for poetry. We used typewriters and letterpress machines to print poetry journals and publications. I remember *Southwestern Colorful Rain* and *Mountain Eagle Soul* as two of our more influential journals. I dare say, I was the most active campus poet in Sichuan during the mid- to late '80s. During my graduation in 1988, I organized a poetry exhibition with two poet classmates.

Yes, at that time we'd already defined ourselves as poets. I even published the poems I wrote during my university years. This, my first unofficial poetry collection, was hand-typeset by my father. In reality I'd become, or at least was very willing to become, a poet who lives and writes by her dreams.

PEMBA AND SZE-LORRAIN: *Which poets have influenced you the most? Are they Chinese or Tibetan poets or others?*

WOESER: During the early years of my poetry writing, the Chinese poetry scene was experiencing revolutionary changes. In my short story "My Twin Sister [Budan]," I described the impact of this huge influence on me:

> Considering external unrest, a huge flag soars in that stormy era while tides surge under the flag: worldwide wanderings and experiences, writings or debates day and night, a strangely nervous rebel, fright, and passion, passion, the mute vanishing, 40 degrees feverish passion, how promising! Almost overnight, years of Budan's unconsciously collected sentiments, that bag of explosives in her little chest, is suddenly lit up by poetry's fatal matchstick and explodes, exploding her into pieces that can no longer be pieced back together.

To clarify, what most influenced the rebellious young Chinese poets then were European, American, and South American contemporary poets, as well as Russian modern poets. This was the case for me too. Rebellious unorthodox poets were my idols. I accepted a few non-Chinese contemporary poets as influences, for example the Irish poet Yeats; from the States, Ginsberg and the Beat poets as well as Plath and the Confessional poets; Russian poets Mandelstam, Akhmatova and Tsvetaeva, etc. The list was endless. After my college graduation, most of the poetry I read was theirs.

Around the same time, I read poems by the Sixth Dalai Lama, Tsangyang Gyatso, and Milarepa. But I read their Chinese translations, the earliest Chinese versions, which are classically very elegant.

PEMBA AND SZE-LORRAIN: *Themes such as travel, Lhasa, memory, and loss recur in your poems. Would you say that these subjects inspire you? Where and how do you seek inspiration?*

WOESER: For me, writing poetry is like searching for memories of a past life. In the epilogue for my poetry collection, *The Whiteness of the Snowland* (Tangshan Publishing House, 2009), I wrote,

> I've always wanted to be a poet. This is the karmic force from a previous life and a continuation of cause and effect. That spring, when I finally returned to the Lhasa I left twenty years ago, I told myself that the only

reason I returned was to hear the voice of that karmic force. For a while, I was very superstitious, thinking that words in some verses might be secret codes, like Ali Baba's *Open Sesame*. I thought that if I keep on writing, a hidden door would suddenly open; that another world—a genuinely kind world—would belong to us all.

I returned to Lhasa in 1990. I was twenty-four. The biggest problem I faced was discovering that the "sinicized" me had become a stranger in her own hometown. This led me into a profound identity crisis. At one point, I thought I'd resolved this problem; a poet friend of mine said, "Actually we're of no nationality. Our identity is poet." His words relieved me to the extent that during the first few years of my stay in Lhasa, I shut myself up in the "ivory tower" of poetry. The poems I wrote became more individualized, with a highly individualized feel, imagination, and language. I thought that poets and artists could tower above all, surpass all national attributes. But writing such poetry didn't alleviate inner turmoil. I can't say that I was suffering terribly. It was probably more of a feeling of emptiness. But I couldn't go on writing this kind of poetry.

When did I leave this "ivory tower"? Travel experiences within vast Tibet changed me gradually: I slowly became intimate with Buddhism and realized clearly how my inner world enriched itself day by day. Amdo, Ü-Tsang, Kham . . . I visited many places, both as a voyager and as a pilgrim. In my heart, I saw the vast snowy land as a gigantic monastery of nature! Of course this was my earliest motivation for the journey. As I walked deeper into the vast snowy land and paused longer, those literary sentiments were gradually replaced by a vocation and a sense of history. I used to see my hometown from just an aesthetics point of view, but I now began to see its people and events with an eye toward history and reality.

In "My Poetry Aesthetics" from *The Whiteness of the Snowland*, I wrote,

Living in a Tibet that has lived through many changes, basking in her sunlight that is especially brilliant in the midst of unfathomable transformations, I slowly feel and realize the benevolence and wisdom of Tibetan Buddhism; slowly see and hear the glory and suffering in Tibetan history and reality . . . All these proffer me a mission: to tell the world about the secret of Tibet.

PEMBA AND SZE-LORRAIN: *"December," "Panchen Lama," and "Secret Tibet" are clearly three political poems about Tibet. Later, you also wrote "The Fear in Lhasa" and "Only This Useless Poem—for Lobsang Tsepak." How much does the political inform your poetry, and has this changed since you started writing? Is it something you are aware of when you write?*

WOESER: "December" was a turning point for me. It was the first poem I wrote from outside the ivory tower. As I said, at that time I was evolving.

In my book of prose *Notes on Tibet*, I wrote, "But being part of the Tibetan people, my spine feels the oppression of a rock-like silhouette of the vast yet suffering Tibet. Between 'glory' and 'helplessness,' I can only choose one of them. It's an 'either-or' case! And what I see as glory isn't merely the 'glory' of a poet but the glory of conscience."

A person of conscience needs to face reality and history. Yet reality and history are very harsh. As a poet in Tibet, I could feel the tension between reality and history in every instant. In the end, this tension shattered the ivory tower that sheltered me. And one day in December 1995, I couldn't help but write "December" on the spot. (It's interesting that this poem was subsequently featured in several official publications, as if no one had understood):

DECEMBER

1

"Hear ye!" The big lie shall blot the sky,
Two sparrows in the wood shall fall.
"Tibet," he says, "Tibet is fine and flourishing!"
The furious girl will not bite her tongue.
Everywhere the monastic robe has lost its color.
They say: It's to save our skin.

But that one, oh,
The steaming blood poured out, the hot blood!
In the next life, who will grieve for him?

2

Storm clouds! Doom!
In my mind's eye I see.

I know if I don't speak now
I'll be silent forever.

Sullen millions,
Lift up your hearts.

He was sacrificed once,
That man of deep red hue.

But as the tree of life is evergreen,
A soul is always a soul.

3
A worse defeat!
Thousands of trees, blighted as never before.
The little folk are quiet as a cricket in the cold.

The pair of praying hands
Was chopped off
To cram the bellies of kites and curs.

Oh, that rosary unseen,
Who is worthy with a firm hand
To pick it up from the slime of this world?

  —December 1995, Lhasa[2]

After I wrote this poem, my poetry actually started to touch on reality and history and began to engage in a narrative style. This is what I wrote in my essay:

> I finally see the clear purpose of my writing, which is to be a witness, to see, to discover, to reveal, and to spread the secret—the shocking, touching yet impersonal secret. Let me also tell stories. Let me use the most commonly seen language—a language that can update definitions, purify and even make new discoveries—to tell stories: the story of Tibet.

PEMBA AND SZE-LORRAIN: *How did you feel when* Notes on Tibet *was banned by the Chinese government? Did it come as a surprise or were you expecting it? Did that experience affect your approach to poetry?*

WOESER: Ah, to be honest, when *Notes on Tibet* was banned, I was a little shocked. I'm actually very slow in certain aspects, thinking that others would understand the stories I wrote; that they would not be banned because they were true stories. This shows that I'm really rather foolish. In fact, after *Notes on Tibet* was completed, a few major publishing houses in Beijing had read the manuscript and greatly appreciated my writing. However, they all asked me to delete certain passages and edit certain words in order to publish the work. Although at that time I was very willing to be published in Beijing, I was not willing to adopt their editorial suggestions. This was why the manuscript was held up for more than a year in some presses in Beijing, before it was sent to a famous publisher in Guangzhou in 2002.

My editor thought my writing was as beautiful as poetry, but interestingly, she did not even know who the Dalai Lama was. (Of course things are different today. After the 2008 unrest in Tibet, due to the Chinese government's demonizing propaganda, most Chinese today know the Dalai Lama as the "devil in a monk's robe.") The ban of *Notes on Tibet* shocked her, and she was subjected to several rounds of self-criticism.

The ban on *Notes on Tibet* and the subsequent ban on *Map of Maroon Red*, published in Beijing the year after, are important turning points in my writing and my life. Together, they signified my turn from unconscious realist writing to conscious realist writing. But what remains unchanged is the beauty of language as my pursuit in writing.

PEMBA AND SZE-LORRAIN: *Two of our favorite poems are "Derge" and "The Prayer Beads of Fate," which are dedicated to or about your father. How did his death impact your writings? Did he share your love of literature, and was he supportive of your path as a writer?*

WOESER: My father did not quite understand my poetry at the beginning. But he was very encouraging.

My first official poetry collection, *Tibet Above*, came out from Qinghai People's Publishing Press in 1999. I burned every page of the book at my father's tomb. Flames swept away each and every black character as if the poems they composed were carried off to another world. I knew he would be relieved, comforted by the fact that I'd become a recognized poet, even if he couldn't understand the poeticism.

But the poems I now write, especially "Tibet's Secret": My father would have understood them right away. But what might he say? Would he still let me continue writing poems? After all, I took a different path.

Later on, my father might have foreseen that writing poetry would change his daughter into someone else, into the kind of person he worried about, so he didn't quite wish to let me continue writing poetry. He'd have rather I become a journalist, a photojournalist, a news journalist . . . To be a poet is too dangerous. But I didn't heed his words. He'd often warn me to "walk with two legs," meaning to go ahead and walk the path I'd chosen, but also walk the path designated by my society and environment. One leg to walk my own road, the other to walk the road that most take. I asked in return, "If we walk with two legs, will one of them break eventually?" He didn't answer.

Perhaps it could be as what poet Derek Walcott, Nobel Prize Laureate in 1992, who grew up during British colonial rule, once wrote:

I who am poisoned with the blood of both,
Where shall I turn, divided to the vein?
I who have cursed
The drunken officer of British rule, how choose
Between this Africa and the English tongue I love?
Betray them both, or give back what they give?
How can I face such slaughter and be cool?
How can I turn from Africa and live?[3]

I wasn't sure if I could express myself lucidly yet. Anyway, I had too many dreams. The most compelling dream was to write a book. In the book, I'd always be a daughter, a daughter who loves her father deeply. I'd have many questions for him, the most urgent being: *Has the path I'm taking now betrayed you? If you were still alive today, would you be angry with me?* On the other hand, I stubbornly believe that, who knows, he might be secretly happy that I'd fulfilled a secret wish of his.

PEMBA AND SZE-LORRAIN: *You published your father's photographs in* Forbidden Memory: Tibet During the Cultural Revolution. *Now that the book has been translated and published in different languages, how do you feel about sharing his "secret photographs" in public?*

WOESER: First of all, I need to make it clear that these photographs of the Cultural Revolution in Tibet are highly sensitive in China, both when I wrote this book, when it was first published in 2006, and today still. Although the book has been translated into Tibetan, Japanese, and English, it remains banned in China. The Chinese version appears only in traditional Chinese characters and not in simplified Chinese. Not only can the book not be published in China, neither can it be mailed from Taiwan or get through customs. I know that hundreds of copies of *Forbidden Memory* have been confiscated by Chinese customs. Dozens of copies sent to me by the Taiwanese publisher Locus Publishing were confiscated.

So the venues mentioned in the question are actually limited and only outside China. And in this huge country of China, the public arena is nonexistent. I think it is an important reminder not to equate China under the CCP with a global readership with public arenas.

PEMBA AND SZE-LORRAIN: *We are sorry to learn that your mother passed away during the COVID-19 confinement... How have you been coping with grief given the current situation in China?*

WOESER: The authorities announced a new COVID outbreak in Lhasa on August 7, 2022. My mother died on the night of August 11. The next day, on August 12, Lhasa went into lockdown.

Since my mother's death and Lhasa's lockdown, I began to record as much news as possible every day, as well as my personal experiences and feelings. I've written 250,000 characters to date, and continue my documentation. I recently started rereading my diary to turn it into a book, but the process was very painful. I think it will probably take me a few months just to sort through this diary. At least half of the texts should be cut. I'll title it *Notes from a Double Epidemic*. The "epidemic" refers not only to diseases but also to disasters. As the medieval historian John Aberth wrote in his *Plagues in World History* (2011), *plague* itself can refer to a particular disease. The word originated from Latin, meaning *thump* or *wound*. In the Old Latin context, *plague* is often associated with some kind of misfortune or disaster, not necessarily a disease. For me, what I've experienced is a double misfortune, a double disaster: the loss of my mother, hit by an epidemic.

Having experienced this double epidemic, every cell in my body is sad, but it's a sadness that only I can experience. It is impossible to use it as a "political tool." Grief should be personal. It's private. I find it hard to talk about it. It's like crying late in the night—it's impossible for others to see. As Roland Barthes said in his diary about his late mother, "I know now that my grief will be chaotic." My grief is similarly beyond measure.

Ultimately it isn't even about feeling sad or not. In the diary I kept for more than a hundred days of lockdown, I wrote,

> It was three a.m. I finished watching a film on my computer and drinking red wine. It was dark outside. The whole city was silent, the mood unsettling. I logged on to Twitter and found a message from an independent journalist who'd been repeatedly silenced by the Chinese authorities: *Lhasa isn't yet unlocked. We still want to write a piece about Lhasa under lockdown... Just write about lockdown life, record it objectively, and... Someone from the Lhasa Cycling Club mentioned that everyone in his community compound was infected, but it was okay, everyone was fine... The cyclist told the most basic truth: Even though infected, nothing happened, yet the compound was sealed off.*

Caught up in my emotions after the film and wine, I responded,

> It isn't about being [COVID] positive or negative, or whether people are recovering or not. That isn't the "truth," as you know. Last night,

I watched the film *Argentina, 1985* and tonight, the film adaptation of Zweig's novella *Chess Story*. These are stories about our mental state, relating to the tortured human spirit in our troubled yet absurd reality. When we haven't personally experienced abuse, we would imagine it possible to preserve human dignity...I was deeply moved by the prosecutor's words in the Argentinian film: *Sadism isn't a political ideology or a tactic of war but moral corruption.* Truth is, everyone in our country of Sodom suffers from such sadism, not just me in Lhasa or someone else in Ürümchi...Unless we have faith, it's difficult to preserve human dignity.

I've noticed how many people, myself included, tend to use words such as *dilemma, prisoner, prison,* and *release* to describe our days of "silent lockdown." I find this noteworthy. Many lives have silently come to an abrupt end; the sound of jumping off a building is extremely disturbing but also fleeting. Sadists still live on, yet the mental anguish they inflict upon the people goes from the so-called three days to three months, three years, and possibly more...

PEMBA AND SZE-LORRAIN: *A lot has changed during these years of Xi, to say the least. America is in its post-Trump period. How do you continue to stay optimistic? What about your faith in storytelling? How far do you think a political story can travel when it can't even reach the ears of those nearby and those who ought to listen?*

WOESER: I'm not an optimist. My hopes for humanity or life, for this or that, is essentially not about Trump. It's nothing to do with Xi or the United States or China. But I've always been interested in stories. I'm a storyteller. Be it writing poetry, prose, reviews, or novels, I'm someone who writes stories. I don't think of a story as "political" or not, but whether it is related to life and destiny. Frankly, so-called political stories only frustrate me.

In the article "The Urgency and Importance of Eyewitness Testimonies" (2015), I quote the French writer Claude Mouchard from his book *When I Shout—Testimonial Literature of the 20th Century*:

The most bitter historical incidents have all been related to state violence. Against this backdrop, to be a so-called "witness" means to report on organized, large-scale political violence from the point of view of those who lived through it. On the most fundamental level, an "eyewitness" is a "survivor," subjected to such forms of violence and supposed to be devoured or deprived of speech, perished in silence. So the language of testimony is naturally one of a new life that still exists and survives despite having been previously wiped away.

I was moved by this passage. My stories—poems, essays, commentaries, historical surveys, oral interviews—are part of this "testimonial literature." They resist the forgetting imposed by those in power. And I hope to use my own writing to break free from the *damnatio memoriae* imposed by colonizers— the state and nationalists, the powerful and the ones authorized by those in power. Evil has always existed and continues to multiply, just as suffering has always existed and continues to multiply. It isn't "something that's never existed before," much less being destroyed or altered by "condemning memory."

Of course, I sometimes wonder if readers out there are willing to listen to my "testimonial stories." But since walking out of the "ivory tower" of poetry, I've believed that writing is to travel, to pray, to witness. But now, I find the idea of travel too light, too pleasant, too romantic. So much suffering and fear exists in reality that writing is far from travel: It is more like an exile. To this end, I've revised the sentence to read: Writing is an exile, a prayer, a testimonial. I believe in this philosophy and am convinced that writing has its value. I don't care how many people want to listen, or even if any do. I don't write to move the "mainstream."

PEMBA AND SZE-LORRAIN: *Back to your writing: How do you think your poetry style has changed over the years?*

WOESER: This brings to mind an email from my husband Wang Lixiong when we first met. His words had a huge impact on me, enough to upheave my "art-for-art's-sake" writing. He said, "Tibet's present plight is sorrowful, but to a writer who documents it, it is the perfect timing. So many legends, acts of bravery, betrayals, falls, longings, separations, as well as the mourning and hope of an ancient people survive around you . . . You can write poetry and novels, but don't forget to turn more of your attention to nonfiction work. That could be even more meaningful for your people."

Also, for me, in terms of my present-day form and writing style, I'm slowly actualizing the self-expression of a "Tibetan identity." This identity is closely interlinked with Tibetan geography, history and culture, as well as countless Tibetans' life stories and fate.

Yes, identity and autobiography, biography as well as the biography of an entire nation is closely connected, otherwise where should we begin as far as the question of identity? In terms of individual narration or renarration of others' life experiences, it is also a way of regaining individual and collective memories. Memory is the most important—because memory is the survival basis for an individual or a collective. When we insist on continuously remembering with all our efforts, our old anxieties will falter. You can say that, at least for me, renarrating life experiences is also a form of therapy.

PEMBA AND SZE-LORRAIN: *In a country and culture that practice collective amnesia, memory must fight its way to survive. But is memory the truth? We each have our own versions of truth, to loosely quote the veteran journalist Bob Woodward, but there are facts. How do you deal with the subjective memory?*

WOESER: Subjective memory? I don't think the stories I write are subjective memories but "testimonial literature," including my unfinished family story, which I've been writing for eighteen years. In order to write it, I visited my father's, my mother's, and my grandparents' hometowns. I interviewed many elders in my family. I collected dozens of hours of recordings alone. The archives of old photos, coupled with the photos I took, were too many to count. It's precisely because I as a documentarist understand the direct relationship between memory and facts that I'm particularly careful about everyone's memory. I've spent so many years writing a book that's closely related to myself, my relatives and family. This is how I process memory or testimony.

PEMBA AND SZE-LORRAIN: *Please describe your daily routine, before and after the pandemic.*

WOESER: Before the pandemic, I was followed and monitored by national security guards every day. They followed even when I was just accompanying my mother to the hospital. But during the pandemic, they disappeared. Lhasa has been "isolated" for more than a hundred days: I can't go out, they can't go out; I have to do PCR tests [medical tests involving polymerase chain reaction] every day, and they too. I was infected by COVID testers who came to do PCR tests at home during the lockdown, and they might have been infected by the same testers too.

A few days after the end of the lockdown in Lhasa, the whole of China was suddenly released from lockdown. The entire country slumped into a situation of forced infection due to the lack of preventative measures, much less drugs and vaccines. Those who were able to pull through their infections recovered, and those who couldn't died suddenly. Lhasa is once again in danger, the number of dead has increased dramatically, and we are once again cautious, still afraid to take off our masks. The national security guards too—so for now, they aren't back to monitor me. How paradoxical. The pandemic seems to have returned some freedom to me.

PEMBA AND SZE-LORRAIN: *For a while, it seemed as though you wrote less poetry but more articles and essays for your blog and books. Why? Do you miss writing poetry?*

WOESER: I've always believed I'm a poet. To a certain extent, I've always been writing poems. Regardless of prose, a hybrid essay or novel, I always believe it to be poetry. In Chinese, the character *poetry* 诗 is composed of *speech* 言 and *temple* 寺. This also means that a poet is an orator: an orator who at the same time has a mission, upholds an aesthetic, and shares religious sentiments. Thus, to be a poet also means to be a witness and memoirist, so as to become an orator of authority.

In writing, inspiration or talent is the same thing, whereas a professionalized working method is a way of normalizing one's working situation. Today, I don't rely merely on the occasional flashes of inspiration. Of course poets have different aesthetics in response to beauty, and through writing, they weave it into words. So I believe I'm always writing poetry and have never stopped doing so.

Deep down in my heart, I've a personal reason. As I wrote in the epilogue for my collection *The Whiteness of the Snowland,*

> A poem comes to my mind, not one of mine but one written by Tibet's greatest poet, the Sixth Dalai Lama Tsangyang Gyatso. I really love this poem:
>
> > Small black letters, written,
> > Vanish with water drop.
> > Mind pictures, unwritten,
> > Though effaced, will not fade.[4]
>
> Dear father Tsering Dorje, the poem I want to dedicate to you is still being written. Because the voice I'm longing to hear is in the air, about to land. In the end you will be relieved to know: When that voice finally lands in the heart, only then is the true poet formed like the dousing of the fire phoenix!

PEMBA AND SZE-LORRAIN: *Lately you've been able to spend much more time in Lhasa, but there was a time of many years when you weren't permitted to visit Lhasa. What are your thoughts on the city now? Do you see yourself spending more time in Lhasa or Beijing in the future?*

WOESER: It's a long story. I stayed for three months in Lhasa in 2014, and after that I was not allowed to return to Lhasa until April 2018. I left Lhasa in October 2018 and was again not allowed to return, not until August 2021. Each time I returned to Lhasa, I had to repeatedly "communicate" with the state apparatus and yet, after finally getting approval, the moment I arrived in Lhasa, I had to accept their face-to-face warnings, "follow up" and be monitored every day, and "drink tea" from time to time.

When I returned to Lhasa at the end of August 2021, they allowed me to stay for three months. But during this time, my mother had an accident: She fell and suffered a fracture, and was taken ill. I took care of her until she passed away in August 2022. I stayed on to settle things after my mother's death, but in two weeks, I'll return to Beijing before returning again in June 2023 . . .

As for the future, I should spend more time living in Beijing. Since my mother's passing, I may not be so eager to return to Lhasa. I need quiet time to write. I don't want "them" to disturb me.

What do I think of Lhasa? Lhasa, forever my deepest love, is also the most heartbreaking, sorrowful, and joyful. A unique lost paradise in this world, falling and mutating. But its heart still beats: Every Wednesday, Sa Lhakpa, Lhakar,[5] mulberry smoke fills the city, silent prayers float to the Potala Palace.

NOTES

1. Translated by Fiona Sze-Lorrain.

2. See Tsering Woeser, *Tibet's True Heart*, trans. A. E. Clark (Dobbs Ferry, NY: Ragged Banner Press, 2008), 12.

3. See Derek Walcott, "A Far Cry from Africa," in *Selected Poems* (New York: Farrar, Straus and Giroux, 2007), 6.

4. See *Songs of Love, Poems of Sadness: The Erotic Verse of the Sixth Dalai Lama*, trans. Paul Williams (London: I. B. Tauris, 2005).

5. "Sa Lhakpa" means "Wednesday," and "Lhakar" means "White Wednesday." "Sa Lhakpa, Lhakar" is the holy White Wednesday associated with His Holiness the Dalai Lama.

ACKNOWLEDGMENTS

"Rinchen the Sky-Burial Master" first appeared in *Sky Lanterns: New Poetry from China, Formosa, and Beyond*, edited by Frank Stewart and Fiona Sze-Lorrain (University of Hawai'i/Mānoa, 2012). "Garpon La's Offerings" first appeared in *On Freedom: Spirit, Art, and State*, also edited by Stewart and Sze-Lorrain (University of Hawai'i/Mānoa, 2013), and was anthologized in *The Penguin Book of Modern Tibetan Essays*, edited by Tenzin Dickie (Vintage, 2023).

Fiona Sze-Lorrain and Dechen Pemba would like to extend their gratitude to Tsering Woeser for her unfailing trust and patience over the years despite geographical distance and censored communication; Christina Cook for her invaluable helping hand and generosity; Tsering Shakya, Philippe Lorrain, Kunsang Kelden, Yangkyi Dolma, Elizabeth Haylett Clark, William C. Sharpe, Morris Rossabi, and Robert Barnett; Tenzin Tsundue and Bhuchung D. Sonam for their support in the early stages of this manuscript; Carole MacGranahan, Tsewang and Lhakpa Pemba, and two much-missed friends, the late Elliot Sperling and Puntsok Tsering; as well as Miriam Angress, Gisela Fosado, Alejandra Mejía, and colleagues at Duke University Press for making this book possible.

GLOSSARY OF PLACE-NAMES

Place-Name	Tibetan	Tibetan (Wylie)	Chinese (Simplified)	Chinese (Pinyin)
Amdo	ཨ་མདོ།	A mdo	安多	Anduo
Chamdo	ཆབ་མདོ།	chab mdo	昌都	Changdu
Chushul	ཆུ་ཤུར།	chu shur	曲水	Qushui
Dappa	འདབ་པ།	'dab pa	稻城	Daocheng
Dartsedo	དར་རྩེ་མདོ།	dar rtse mdo	康定	Kangding
Drigung Til Monastery	འབྲི་གུང་མཐིལ།	'bri gung mthil	直贡梯寺	Zhigongti Si
Gonjo	གོ་འཇོ།	go 'jo	贡觉	Gongjue
Horra	ཧོར་ར།	hor ra	柯拉	Kela
Jyekundo	སྐྱེ་རྒུ་མདོ།	skye rgu mdo	玉树	Yushu
Kham	ཁམས།	khams	康	Kang
Lhasa	ལྷ་ས།	lha sa	拉萨	Lasa
Lithang	ལི་ཐང་།	li thang	理塘	Litang
Meldro Gungkar	མལ་གྲོ་གུང་དཀར།	mal gro gung dkar	墨竹工卡	Mozhugongka
Ngari	མངའ་རིས།	mnga' ris	阿里	Ali
Nyakchuka	ཉག་ཆུ་ཁ།	nyag chu kha	雅江	Yajiang
Nyarong	ཉག་རོང་།	nyag rong	新龙	Xinlong
Ombu	ཚོམ་བུ།	'om bu	文部	Wenbu
Palyul	དཔལ་ཡུལ།	dpal yul	白玉	Baiyu
Palyul Monastery	དཔལ་ཡུལ་དགོན།	dpal yul dgon	白玉寺	Baiyu Si
Pangpu Monastery	སྤང་ཕུག་དགོན།	spang phug dgon	蚌普寺	Bengpu Si
Sakya Monastery	ས་སྐྱ་དགོན།	sa skya dgon	萨迦寺	Sajia Si

(continued)

Place-Name	Tibetan	Tibetan (Wylie)	Chinese (Simplified)	Chinese (Pinyin)
Sera Monastery	སེ་ར་དགོན།	se ra dgon	色拉寺	Sela Si
Tashi Lhunpo Monastery	བཀྲ་ཤིས་ལྷུན་པོ།	bkra shis lhun po	扎什伦布寺	Zhashi Lunbu Si
Tibet Autonomous Region	བོད་རང་སྐྱོང་ལྗོངས།	bod rang skyong ljongs	西藏自治区	Xizang Zizhiqu
Toelung Dechen	སྟོད་ལུང་བདེ་ཆེན།	stod lung bde chen	堆龙德庆	Duilongdeqing
Tsurphu Monastery	མཚུར་ཕུ་དགོན།	mtshur phu dgon	楚布寺	Chubu Si
Ü-Tsang	དབུས་གཙང་།	dbus gtsang	卫藏	Weizang

BIBLIOGRAPHY

Tsering Woeser's bibliography contains mainly twenty-three books of fiction, autofiction, lyrical prose, poetry, and oral history, as well as two coauthored volumes of nonfiction. She has to her name twenty books in translation (Catalan, Czech, English, French, German, Japanese, Polish, Spanish, and Tibetan).

BOOKS

Tibet Above [poetry]. Xining: Qinghai People's Publishing, 1999.
Notes on Tibet [lyrical prose]. Guangzhou: Flower City Publishing, 2003 [banned].
Tibet: The Map of Maroon Red [travelogue]. Taipei: Shiying Publishing, 2003.
The Map of Maroon Red [travelogue with illustrations]. Beijing: China Tourism
  Publishing House, 2004 [banned].
Forbidden Memory: Tibet During the Cultural Revolution [oral history and historical images of Tibet during the Cultural Revolution]. Taipei: Locus Publishing,
  2006. Rev. ed., 2023.
Memories of Tibet [oral history of Tibet during the Cultural Revolution]. Taipei: Locus Publishing, 2006.
A Poem of Tibet [rev. ed. of the banned *Notes on Tibet*]. Taipei: Locus Publishing,
  2006.
Prayer Beads Stories [short stories and novellas]. Hong Kong: Strong Wind, 2007.
Invisible Tibet [texts with illustrations]. Taipei: Locus Publishing, 2008.
The Snow Lion Roars in the Year of the Rat [chronicle of the 2008 Tibetan unrest].
  Taipei: Asian Culture Publishing, 2009.
The Whiteness of Snowland [poetry]. Taipei: Tangshan Publishing, 2009.
Tibet: 2008 [stories]. Taipei: Linking Publishing, 2011.
Dossier on Self-Immolation in Tibetan [nonfiction]. Taipei: Snowland Publishing,
  2013.
The Death of Tenzin Delek Rinpoche [nonfiction]. Taipei: Snowland Publishing,
  2015.
The Tibetan Fire Phoenix [nonfiction]. Taipei: Locus Publishing, 2015.

Behind the Paradise [nonfiction]. Taipei: China Times Publishing, 2016.

Forbidden Memory: Tibet During the Cultural Revolution [new commemorative ed. for the fiftieth anniversary of the Cultural Revolution]. Taipei: Locus Publishing, 2016.

The Maroon Red Ruins [hybrid texts]. Taipei: Locus Publishing, 2017.

Endless Space [oral history and interviews]. Taipei: Snowland Publishing, 2018.

Amnye Machen, Amnye Machen [poetry]. Taipei: Snowland Publishing, 2020.

Tibet in the Year of Pandemic [lyrical prose, fiction, poetry]. Taipei: Locus Publishing, 2021.

The Plague [poetry]. Hong Kong: Liker Land, NFT ebook, 2024.

Under the Scorching Sun in Lhasa [poetry]. Taipei and Hong Kong: 2046 Press, 2024.

COAUTHORED BOOKS

Voices from Tibet [political commentary]. Coauthored with Wang Lixiong. Taipei: Locus Publishing, 2009.

Tibet over These Years [political commentary]. Coauthored with Wang Lixiong. Taipei: Asian Culture Publishing, 2012.

BOOKS IN TRANSLATION

Unlocking Tibet [essays, English]. Coauthored with Wang Lixiong. Multiple translators. Zurich: Garuda Books, 2000.

བོད་གདངས་སུ་གྱེར་བའི་སྙན་རྩོམ། *Bod gdangs su gyer ba'i snyan rtsom* [*A Poem of Tibet*; essays and stories, Tibetan]. Translated by Chakmo Tso, Taklha Gyal, and Namlo Yak Lhade. Dharamsala: Multi Education Editing Center, 2002.

Tibet's True Heart [poetry, English]. Translated by A. E. Clark. Dobbs Ferry, NY: Ragged Banner Press, 2008.

El Tibet trenca el seu silenci [*Tibet: Breaking the Silence*; political commentary, Catalan]. Translated by Tenzin Namgyal and Àlvar Valls. Lleida: Pagès Editors, 2008.

གངས་སེང་གི་ངར་སྒྲ། *Gangs seng gi ngar sgra* [*The Snow Lion Roars in the Year of the Rat: A Chronicle of the 2008 Events in Tibet*; nonfiction, Tibetan]. Translated by Kunthar Dhondup. Dharamsala: Tibetan Translation House, 2009.

གསར་བརྗེ། *Gsar brje* [*Forbidden Memory: Tibet During the Cultural Revolution*; nonfiction, Tibetan]. Translated by Dolkar. Oslo: Norwegian Tibet Committee, 2009.

Ihr habt die Gewehre, ich einen Stift [*You Have Guns, I Have a Pen*; nonfiction, German]. Translated by Gottfried Gärtner. Berlin: Lungta Verlag, 2009.

El Tibet rompe su silencio [*Tibet: Breaking the Silence*; political commentary, Spanish]. Translated by Tenzin Namgyal. Lleida and Barcelona: Editorial Milenio, 2009.

殺劫（シャーチェ）チベットの文化大革命 [*Forbidden Memory: Tibet During the Cultural Revolution*; nonfiction, Japanese]. Translated by Fujino Akira and Liu Yanzi. Fukuoka: Shukousha, 2009. Rev. ed., 2025.

Mémoire interdite : Témoignages sur la Révolution culturelle au Tibet [*Forbidden Memory: Tibet During the Cultural Revolution*; nonfiction, French]. Translated by Bernard Bourrit and Li Zhang-Bourrit. Paris: Gallimard, 2010.

チベットの秘密 [*The Secret of Tibet*; essays, Japanese]. Coauthored with Wang Lixiong, translated by Liu Yanzi. Fukuoka: Shukousha, 2012.

Immolations au Tibet — La honte du monde [*Immolations in Tibet: The Shame of the World*; nonfiction, French]. Preface by Robert Badinter, translated by Dekyid. Montpellier: Indigène éditions, 2013.

Niewidoczny Tybet [*Invisible Tibet*; nonfiction, Polish]. Translated by Adam Kozieł. Warsaw: DIALOG, 2013.

Voices from Tibet: Selected Essays and Reportage by Tsering Woeser and Wang Lixiong [nonfiction, English]. Coauthored with Wang Lixiong, introduction by Robert Barnett, translated by Violet S. Law. Honolulu: University of Hawai'i Press, 2013.

Tibet srdce, Tibet mysli [*Tibet of the Heart, Tibet of the Mind*; poetry, Czech]. Translated by Karla Vrátná and Olga Lomová. Prague: PEN Prague, 2014.

Zápisky z Tibetu [*Notes on Tibet*; nonfiction, Czech]. Translated by Kamila Hladíková. Prague: Verzone, 2015.

Tibet on Fire: Self-Immolation Against Chinese Rule [nonfiction, English]. Translated by Kevin Carrico. London: Verso Books, 2016.

Tybet płonie [*Tibet on Fire*; nonfiction, Polish]. Translated by Adam Kozieł. Warsaw: Wydawnictwo Akademickie Dialog, 2016.

Forbidden Memory: Tibet During the Cultural Revolution [nonfiction, English]. Foreword by Wang Lixiong, photographs by Tsering Dorje, edited by Robert Barnett, translated by Susan T. Chen. Lincoln, NE: Potomac Books, 2020.

Amnyé Machen, Amnyé Machen [poetry, French]. Translated by Brigitte Duzan and Valentina Peluso, edited and annotated by Katia Buffetrille. Andert-et-Condon: Éditions Jentayu, 2023.

In addition, individual poems, lyrical essays, short stories, novellas, articles, and political commentaries have been widely anthologized in collections from various Chinese presses, as well as translated into Tibetan, English, French, German, Spanish, Norwegian, Japanese, Finnish, Danish, Catalan, Italian, Bulgarian, and other languages.

BLOGS

Invisible Tibet. http://woeser.middle-way.net.
Map of Maroon Red. http://map.woeser.com/?viewmode=normal.

FEATURE COLUMNS

Radio Free Asia Tibetan Program. http://www.rfa.org/tibetan/chediklaytsen
/ukaylatsen/woser.
Radio Free Asia Woeser's Special Commentaries. https://www.rfa.org/mandarin
/pinglun/weise.
Radio Free Asia Woeser's blog. https://www.rfa.org/mandarin/pinglun/weiseblog.
High Peaks Pure Earth's English translations of Woeser's blog: https://highpeaks
pureearth.com/category/key-voices/woeser/.

HONORS AND AWARDS

2001 Junma Award for Ethnic Literature
2005 Hellman/Hammett International Grant
2006 *China Times* Top Ten Best Chinese Books Award for *Forbidden Memory:
       Tibet During the Cultural Revolution*
2007 "Fearless Speaker" Medal, Association of Tibetan Journalists in India
2007 Freedom of Expression Prize, Norwegian Authors' Union
2007 Neustadt International Prize for Literature [nominated]
2008 Honored/Highlighted by PEN American Center [Day of the Imprisoned Writer]
2009 Hellman/Hammett International Grant
2009 Lin Zhao Memorial Prize, Independent Chinese PEN Center
2010 Courage in Journalism Prize, International Women's Media Foundation
2011 Prince Claus Award, the Netherlands
2012 Premio Reporteros sin Fronteras, BOBS [Best of the Blogs] Award, La Deutsche
       Welle
2013 International Women of Courage Award, US Department of State
2013 Sakharov Prize [nominated]
2014 Award for the Promotion of Sino-Tibetan Civil Exchange [with Wang Lixiong],
       Melbourne Association for the Promotion of Sino-Tibetan Civil Exchange,
       Australia

BIOGRAPHIES

ABOUT THE AUTHOR

Prominent Tibetan poet, essayist, fiction writer, journalist, and human rights activist TSERING WOESER was born in 1966 in Lhasa and had an elite Chinese upbringing. She is the author of multiple volumes of poetry, novellas, and nonfiction, including two of the most significant books in Chinese on Tibet, *Notes on Tibet* (2003) and *Forbidden Memory: Tibet During the Cultural Revolution* (2006). Condemned as a book on a "forbidden subject," her bestselling *Notes on Tibet* was banned upon publication. Woeser faced persecution and censorship and was ordered to self-criticism and confessions. She refused and moved into exile in Beijing. Removed from her post at *Tibetan Literature* and denied her social welfare and passport, she has often been placed under house arrest during "sensitive public occasions." She is still living under social threats and police surveillance in Beijing and Lhasa. Translated into several languages, Woeser's work has appeared in the *New York Times*, the *New York Review of Books*, and the *Washington Post*, among other publications.

ABOUT THE EDITORS/TRANSLATORS AND CONTRIBUTOR

FIONA SZE-LORRAIN is a writer, poet, translator, editor, and zheng harpist who writes and translates in English, French, and Chinese. Her work includes a novel in stories, *Dear Chrysanthemums* (2023); five poetry collections, most recently *Rain in Plural* (2020) and *The Ruined Elegance* (2016); eighteen books of translation, and three coedited anthologies of international literature. A finalist for the Los Angeles Times Book Prize, the Best Translated Book Award, and the Derek Walcott Prize for Poetry, among other honors, she was longlisted for the 2024 Andrew Carnegie Medal for Excellence in Fiction. A judge for the 2025 International Dublin Literary Award and a 2019–20 Abigail R. Cohen Fellow at the Columbia Institute for Ideas and Imagination, she lives in Paris and serves as an editor at Vif Éditions.

DECHEN PEMBA is a UK-born Tibetan who graduated from University College London and the School of Oriental and African Studies, University of London. With over twenty years of experience, she has worked as a lobbyist and campaigner on Tibetan issues and served as a consultant on Tibet-related work for human rights organizations. She has lived in Berlin and Beijing. Currently she resides in London, where she works as a researcher and edits High Peaks Pure Earth, a website that offers translations, news, and commentary from Tibetan internet and social media. She also cocurates the annual Tibet Film Festival and is involved with several Tibet-related projects such as Project Democracy (Smartvote) and The Future of Tibet.

PANKAJ MISHRA is the author of *Run and Hide* (2022), *Age of Anger* (2017), *From the Ruins of Empire* (2012), and six other books of nonfiction and fiction. He is a columnist at *Bloomberg View* and the *New York Times Book Review*, and writes regularly for the *New York Review of Books*, the *Guardian*, the *London Review of Books*, and the *New Yorker*. The recipient of several literary honors, including the Windham-Campbell Literature Prize from Yale, and a fellow of the Royal Society of Literature, he lives in London.

Beijing: Beijing Middle Road, 114, 115; Beijing University for Nationalities, 60; as capital city, vii, 2, 4, 5, 6, 14, 17, 37, 40, 54, 69, 77, 81, 83, 84, 88, 96, 121, 136, 172, 173, 179, 180; Central University for Ethnic Nationalities, 133; Chinese Parliament Two Sessions meeting in, 144; contacts with Dharamsala, 45; declaring martial law in Lhasa, 17; King Birendra's visit, 81; Olympic Games in, 9, 136, 143, 144

Beat poets. *See* American, poets; Ginsberg, Allen

beshing shamo, 22

blog: *Invisible Tibet*, 4; *Map of Maroon Red*, 4, 173, by Snowland Dust, 115

Bodhisattva, 21, 103

Bon: as Tibet's original religion, 65, 72n4; religious teachings, 58; tradition, 60, 67–68; witchcraft, 66. *See also* religion, in Tibetan life

Borges, Jorge Luis, 3

Bouyei (people), 83

Boym, Svetlana, 3, 130n4

Brandishing a Sword in Tibet. See Yang, Haiying

British: black tea, 153; colonialism, 173; Legation, 110

Brodsky, Joseph, 127, 130n6

Browning pistols, 92

Buddha: broken statue fingers in Dalai Lama's collection, 97, 100; Dipamkara, 58, 72n5; ruined statues in Jokhang's courtyard, 97; Saga Dawa, 50n1; smashed, 106; smiling, 17; story of, 29

Buddhism: arrival in Tibet, 66; Nyingma, 150; Tantric, 28; teachings of, 58, 160; Ten Directions, 29; Vajrayana, 147; Woeser's relationship with, 3, 170. *See also* ban, on Buddhism; Drigung Kagyu; Karma Kagyu; religion

businessman, 8, 42, 58, 64, 71n1, 72n2, 121, 142

butter lamps, 18, 33

Cabinet. *See Kashag*

camera: Contax and high-end, 92; digital, 54; for surveillance in streets, 131, 146; used by Tsering Dorje, 91; used by Woeser, 23, 123, 128, 158; Zeiss Ikon, 91

campaign: organized by Karma, 8, 64, 67; Liaoshen, 93

car: armored, 17; in general, 75, 76, 80, 95, 111, 137, 138, 139, 143, 147, 153, 154, 155, 156, 159, 161, 162, 163; Lanxing, 142; police, 137, 138; Toyota Desert King, 57; Toyota SUV, 154; Volkswagen, 151, 154, 161

cashmere, 62, 63. *See also* clothes; sheepskin; wool

caterpillar fungi, 64, 72n13

CCP (Chinese Communist Party): base of, 93; founding fathers, 92; invasion, 87, 132n1; official, 47, 69, 71, 72n1, 76, 79, 82, 116, 140, 141, 143; People's Commune, 59, 116; raids, 96; slogans, 30, 83, 97; Tibetan members, 97. *See also* army, Eighth Route

censorship, 4, 5, 9. *See also* ban

Chadey Karpo, 38

Chakpori Hill, 144

Chairman Mao. *See* Mao, Zedong

Chamdo, 61, 71n1, 89, 109

Changchun, 93

Changseshar. *See* Yabzhi Taktser

Changtang, 138

Charter 08, 6

Chen, Yi, 92. *See also* CCP (Chinese Communist Party)

Chen, Zonglie, 88

Chengdu, 1, 14, 15, 16, 54, 63, 64, 65. *See also* Sichuan

Chenghua District Government, 63, 64

Chenrezig (Buddha of Compassion), 48, 98. *See also* Bodhisattva

Chess Story. See Zweig, Stefan

Chiang, Kai-shek, 94

Chinese: authorities/officials, 3, 7, 71, 127, 140, 146, 175; books on Tibet, 1; civil war, 93; colonial policies in Tibet, 69; currency, 34n2, 94, 96; delegates to UN, 68; friendship with Nepal, 83; language, 1, 9, 17, 87, 104n9, 167, 174; nationalist hackers, 4; Parliament in Beijing, 144. *See also* CCP (Chinese Communist Party)

Chingdrol Magmi. *See* armed forces, People's Liberation Army (PLA)

Chodrak, 21–25, 30, 31–34

Choekyi, 101

Chushul County, 80

circumambulation, 18, 61, 109, 153, 165

clothes: brocade gown, 41; *Changdi*, 44; *chuba*, 111; in general, 15, 36, 54, 57, 62, 63, 69, 82, 121, 138, 140, 157; *khata*, 21, 35, 37n1, 69–71, 79, 89, 100; leather, 81; overcoat, 24; *pagtsag*, 151, 156; robe, 26, 31, 73, 111, 138, 141, 154, 171, 173. *See also* cashmere; sheepskin; wool

collective amnesia, 178. *See also* memory; truth

compassion, 20, 29, 47, 48n5, 49, 66, 72, 101, 105n14, 161. *See also* Avalokiteshvara (Bodhisattva of Compassion); Chenrezig (Buddha of Compassion)

Confessional poets. *See* American, poets; Plath, Sylvia

corpse, 19, 25, 28, 29, 33, 34, 62, 126. *See also* sky burial

Courage in Journalism Prize. *See* International Women's Media Foundation

Covid 19: lockdown in Lhasa, 5, 174, 175, 178; PCR tests, 178; zero-Covid policy, 6

cultural assimilation, 14

Cultural Revolution: after, 29, 103; death, destruction, and difficulties during, 45, 61, 88, 91, 103; King Birendra's visit during, 82; Lhasa during, 41, 45, 91, 97, 102, 104n9, 113, 116; in Nyemo, 132n1; and smashed Buddha, 106; and sky burials, 29. *See also* Tsering Woeser, *individual works, Forbidden Memory: Tibet During the Cultural Revolution*

currency. *See* Chinese, currency; *tangka. See also* money; ocean; Shenyang Mint

Dabpa County, 20

damma, 39, 46, 47. *See also* Gar; music

Dai (people). *See* Songkran festival

dakini: of Guru Rinpoche, 28, 158, 162n5–6; *shasa khandro*, 28, 29

Dalai Lama: clans of, 109; the Fifth, 43; the Sixth, 16, 169, 179, 180n4; residence at Potala, 109, 118; the Thirteenth, 108, 110

Dalai Lama the Fourteenth: brothers of, 88, 129; leaving for exile (March 17, 1959); 104n5, 110, 123; meeting Garpon La, 46; niece of, 129; Nobel Peace Prize, 100; sister of, 128; written account in *Dharamsala Mahayana Buddhist Tsulagkhang Historical Records*, 98. *See also* individual works

Freedom in Exile (Dalai Lama), 93

My Land and My People (Dalai Lama), 93

dance: bonfire, 16; Dalai Lama's troupe, 42; folk, 83; party, 162; tap, 35. *See also* Gar

Dartsedo, 1, 17n1, 20, 21

dayang. See ocean

deity, 47, 66. *See also* Dolma, Ekajata; gods; goddess; Goddess Tara; spirit

Jetsun Pema. *See* Dalai Lama the Fourteenth, sister of

jewelry, 42, 92, 95, 100, 111, 163. *See also* gold; silver

Jiang, Zemin, 82, 83–84, 85

Jiangsu Province, 104n9

Jiangxi Province, 106

Johnson, Ian. *See* journal, *individual publications, New York Review of Books*

Jokhang Temple, 17, 33, 61, 72n10, 91, 97, 100, 102, 105n10, 140. *See also* Tukje Lhakhang

journal: journalism, 2, 3, 6, 7; journalist, 1, 5, 6, 7, 23, 70, 77, 79, 88, 89, 101, 134, 139, 167, 173, 175; literary, 1, 16, 167; musical, 40. *See also individual publications*

Cerise Press, 3, 167

Mountain Eagle Soul, 168

New York Review of Books, 6

Southwestern Colorful Rain, 168

Tibetan Literature, 1, 4, 16

Jowo Rinpoche, 33, 34

ka year, 45, 48n2

Kafka, Franz, 3

Kagyu school. *See* Drigung Kagyu; Karma Kagyu

Kangding, 10n1, 14, 16, 17n1. *See also* Dartsedo

Kardze, 1, 104n1, 138

karma, 49, 58, 59, 72n8, 155, 159–61

Karma Kagyu, 34n4

Karma Kuchen Rinpoche. *See* Rinpoche, Karma Kuchen

Karma Samdrup, 71n1. *See also dzi*

kasaya, 53

Kashag, 111

Kasho Dhondup, 88

Kazara, 97, 98, 105n13

Kerry, John, 6

Kham: Khampa, 58, 59, 68, 71, 72n6; as place, 1, 7, 20, 21, 23, 54, 55, 56, 58, 64, 65, 71n1, 89, 121, 140, 141, 170; Tibetan, 56, 58

Khando. *See* Dalai Lama the Fourteenth, niece of

Khandroma, 158, 162n5. *See also dakini*; Rinpoche, Guru

khata, 21, 35, 37n1, 69, 70, 71, 79, 89, 100

Khrushchev, Nikita, 85

killing, 104n4, 144, 147, 155, 158, 160, 161

Kim, Jong-il, 85

King Birendra of Nepal, 75, 80–83, 84, 85. *See also* Nepal

King Gesar. *See* Gesar

King Songtsen Gampo, 100, 105n11

Kirti Monastery. *See* monastery, Kirti

knife, 13, 19, 25, 26, 28

Kohl, Helmut. *See* Germany, Chancellor's 1987 visit to Tibet

Ksitigarbha Sutra, 3

Kundun. *See* Dalai Lama and Dalai Lama the Fourteenth

kyang, 80, 86n1

Kyichu River, 41

labor camp. *See* Gormo labor camp

Ladakh, 43

Laird, Thomas, 101

lama, 8, 20, 24, 25, 26, 34n3, 58, 61, 62, 88, 111, 130n1–2, 148, 152, 158. *See also* Dalai Lama; Dalai Lama the Fourteenth

language: body, 74; of expression, 2; Han Chinese, 1, 2, 9, 17, 37, 56, 87, 167, 174; merits, 3; native, 2; Spanish, 56; street slang, 152; of testimony, 176; Tibetan, 2, 16, 17, 56, 80, 108, 174; of Woeser, 8, 170, 173; Yi, 16

leaflet. *See Rules Governing Student Behavior*

legend, 14, 57, 158, 177. *See also* myth

Lenin, Vladimir, 115

ley gyumdey. See karma

Lha-shing, 58. *See also* spirit

Lhakar, 180

Lhalu. *See* Dalai Lama, clans of

performances. *See also* dance; music

Petech, Luciano, 108. *See also* Tibetologist

Phagpala Gelek Namgyal, 109, 130n1

phone: camera, 123; cell, 54, 128, 140; iPhone, 47, 82; line, 32, 151, 152; mobile apps, 4; rotary, 31

photograph: in books, 40, 111; of Dalai Lama, 126; on internet, 19, 79, 115; in propaganda exhibitions, 89, 92; taken by Tsering Dorje, 7, 17, 91, 174; taken by Woeser, 8, 26, 34, 84, 118, 128; unknown source, 109. *See also* picture; portrait

Phunkhang. *See* Dalai Lama, clans of

Phuntsog, 133, 135. *See also* monk

Phuntsok Wangyal, 64, 70

picture, 9, 26, 68, 74, 89, 106, 115, 118, 121, 127, 128, 140, 144, 179. *See also* photograph; portrait

pilgrimage, 33, 61, 62, 65

Plagues in World History. See Aberth, John

Plath, Sylvia, 169

police: armed, 76, 137, 139, 141, 146n1; internet, 7; plainclothes, 74, 131. *See also* armed forces; Jebumgang Police Station

portrait, 21, 97, 117, 123. *See also* photograph; picture

poster, 123, 128, 138, 139, 142

Potala: eastern side of, 110; Potala Palace, 16, 18, 61, 72n9, 82, 105, 109, 110, 112, 115, 118, 121, 126, 129, 131, 140, 144, 145, 146, 180; Potala Square, 144

prayer bead, 51, 52–53, 173. *See also dzi*

Prince Claus Award, 6

propaganda, 89, 138, 142, 173

prostrations, 3, 43

protest, protestor, 4, 17, 69, 134, 143. *See also* hunger strike; resistance; self-immolation

publisher, 3, 39, 172. *See also individual presses*

Locus Publishing, 174

Qinghai People's Publishing Press, 173

Tangshan Publishing House, 169

Tibet Xinhua Publishing House, 39

Qiang, 138

Qinghai Province: highway between Sichuan, Tibet, and, 144; highway between Tibet and, 43, 136, 139; railway between Tibet and, 139, 141; as region, 65, 66, 108, 140, 173

radio: Philips, 92; Radio Free Asia, 5

Rahula, 57

railway: company from Zhejiang, 80; constructed by Gormo prisoners, 43; construction sites for reeducation, 7; Lhasa to Shigatse, 80. *See also* Qinghai Province, railway between Tibet and

reform and economic opening-up, 82

reincarnation, 20, 33, 35, 130n2

religion: county religious affairs bureau, 21; in Tibetan life, 58, 159. *See* Bon; Buddhism; funeral

resistance, 7, 9, 17, 112. *See also* hunger strike; protest, protestor; self-immolation

restaurant, 38, 121, 145. *See also* Dicos; food; tea; teahouse; Turquoise Dumplings

Revolution. *See* teahouse. *See also* food; tea

Rinchen. *See* sky burial, Rinchen

Rinpoche: Guru, 62, 72n11, 100, 157, 158; Gyalwa, 98; Jowo, 33, 34; Karma Kuchen, 20, 29; Ngari, 111; Taktser, 88; Tenzin Delek, 26, 29, 32, 33, 34n3; Woeser and a, 136

Rolex. *See* luxury products

ruins. *See* Yabzhi Taktser

sweet, 36, 152, 154. *See also* British, black tea

teahouse, 152–53. *See also* food; noodles; restaurant; tea

temple, 17, 34, 65, 73, 97, 99, 131, 134, 141, 179. *See also* Jokhang Temple

Tenzin Chodak. *See* Dalai Lama the Fourteenth, brothers of

Tenzin Choegyal. *See* Dalai Lama the Fourteenth, brothers of

Tenzin Delek Rinpoche. *See* Rinpoche, Tenzin Delek

Tenzin Gyatso. *See* Dalai Lama the Fourteenth

Terdrom Hot Spring, 147–52, 156, 158, 159, 161

Terma scriptures, 55

Terton, 68, 72n14

testimonial literature, 176, 178

thangka, 57, 70, 72n3

Three Rivers Environmental Protection Group. *See* environmentalism, environmental protection

Thukje Chempo, 102, 104, 105n14

Tiananmen, 4

Tibet Religious Foundation of the Dalai Lama in Taiwan, 97

Tibet University, 47, 154. *See also* education; Garpon Pasang Dhondup

Tibetan Mansion, Tibetan Pearl Garden Hotel. *See* guesthouse, Second Government

Tibetologist, 58, 78, 108

Toelung Dechen: county, 28; district, 142

toeshey, 40, 44. *See also* Gar; music

Tohti, Ilham, 6

toilet: bowl, 76, 77; for celebrity, 74–75, 84–85; flush, 76, 80, 81, 82, 86

tokden. See sky burial, master

tourism, 9, 22, 137, 144. *See also* Beijing, Olympic Games in; hotel; Terdrom Hot Spring

Traditional Tibetan Medical College, 140. *See also* education; medicine

Tromsikhang, 106. *See also* Barkhor

truck: Isuzu, 62; Jiefang, 61

truth, 8, 9, 128, 151, 175, 178

tsampa. *See* food, tsampa

Tsangyang Gyatso. *See* Dalai Lama the Sixth

Tsarong Dasang Damdul, 100. *See also* aristocrats

Tsering Dorje. *See* Tsering Woeser, father of

Tsering Woeser: cousin of, 147, 151, 152, 155, 161; early life and education, 1–2, 14–17, 167–70; as editor, 1, 16, 167; father of, 1, 7, 14, 17, 39, 90, 168, 173–74, 179; husband of, 6, 96, 136, 138, 157, 177; mother of, 6, 18, 44, 144, 146, 174–75, 178, 180; narrative style of, 3, 7–10; persecution of, 4, 7, 135, 178; social media presence of, 4–5, 175; uncle of, 44. *See also individual works*

Forbidden Memory: Tibet During the Cultural Revolution (Woeser), 1, 6, 7, 118, 174

Notes from a Double Epidemic (Woeser), 175

Notes on Tibet (Woeser), 1, 3, 171, 172–173

Tibet Above (Woeser), 173

Tibet on Fire: Self-Immolation Against Chinese Rule (Woeser), 7

Voices from Tibet (Woeser), 5, 7, 8

The Whiteness of the Snowland (Woeser), 169–170, 179

Tsering Youdon. *See* Tsering Woeser, mother of

tsethar, 162n6

tsongba. See businessman

Tsuglagkhang. *See* Jokhang Temple

Tsurphu River, 28. *See also* monastery, Tsurphu

Tsvetaeva, Marina, 2, 169

tuhao, 95

Tukje Lhakhang. *See* Jokhang Temple

Turquoise Dumplings, 138. *See also* food; restaurant

Ü-Tsang, 40, 74, 80, 85, 170
Ukraine, 4
United Front Work Department, 118
United Nations (UN), 67, 68, 69, 71.
    See also Annan, Kofi
Unity Village. *See* village, Unity
uprising. *See* Lhasa, 1959 uprising/
    massacre in, 1989 uprising in, 2008
    uprising/bloodshed in
US State Department, 6

Vajrayana. *See* Buddhism, Vajrayana
valley, 14, 18, 80, 147. *See also* Yarlung
    Tsangbo Grand Canyon
village, 22, 25, 36, 58, 64, 143, 154. *See
    also individual places*
    Dungkar (New Socialist), 142
    Hongya, 108
    New Shol, 146
    Unity, 38, 43
vultures, 19, 25, 27–29, 33, 49. *See also*
    sky burial

Walcott, Derek, 173, 180n3
wall paintings. *See* murals
Wang, Lixiong. *See* Tsering Woeser,
    husband of. *See also* sky burial, *Sky
    Burial: The Fate of Tibet*
*When I Shout—Testimonial Literature
    of the 20th Century. See* Mouchard,
    Claude
White Wednesday. *See* Lhakar
Woodward, Bob, 178. *See also* journal,
    journalism, journalist
wool, 62, 81, 85, 92, 104n3, 151. *See
    also* cashmere; clothes; sheepskin
World War II, 68

Xianzu Island, 121
Xie, Fangyi, 97
Xinhua News Agency, 82–83
Xining, 59

Yabzhi Taktser, 108–9, 114–28
yak: as animal, 31, 32, 54; butter, 35.
    See also food
Yan'an, 93
Yang, Haiying, 104n2
Yangtze River, 19, 87
Yarlung Tsangbo Grand Canyon, 76,
    85. *See also* valley
Yeats, W. B., 169
Yeshe Tsogyal, 158
Yi: as ethnicity and language, 16
Yida, 66. *See* deity
Yidam, 158. *See also* Rinpoche,
    Guru
Yonru, 32. *See also* Lithang
yuan (*renminbi*, RMB). *See* Chinese,
    currency
Yuan, Shikai, 93, 96–97, 104n8
Yushu Tibetan Autonomous Pre-
    fecture, 66. *See also* Qinghai
    Province

Zhang, Xueliang, 94
Zhapten Monastery. *See* monastery,
    Zhapten
Zhu, Rikun, 5. *See also* film
Zhu, Rongji, 65. *See also* CCP (Chi-
    nese Communist Party)
zhungzhug, 97, 99, 100, 105
Zweig, Stefan, 176